THE NEW CURTAIN BOOK

THE NEW CURTAIN BOOK

master classes with today's top designers

Stephanie Hoppen

photography by Fritz von der Schulenburg

Bulfinch Press
AOL Time Warner Book Group
Boston New York London

To Stuart, who helped make it happen

Text copyright © 2003 by Stephanie Hoppen

Photographs copyright © 2003 by Jacqui Small, an Imprint of Aurum
Press Ltd., and Interior Archive, except photographs listed on page 192

Compilation copyright © 2003 by Jacqui Small

First United States Edition

First printed in Great Britain in 2003 by Jacqui Small, an imprint of
Aurum Press Ltd.

ISBN 0-8212-2827-7

Library of Congress Control Number 2002112078

Bulfinch Press is a division of AOL Time Warner Book Group.

Printed in China

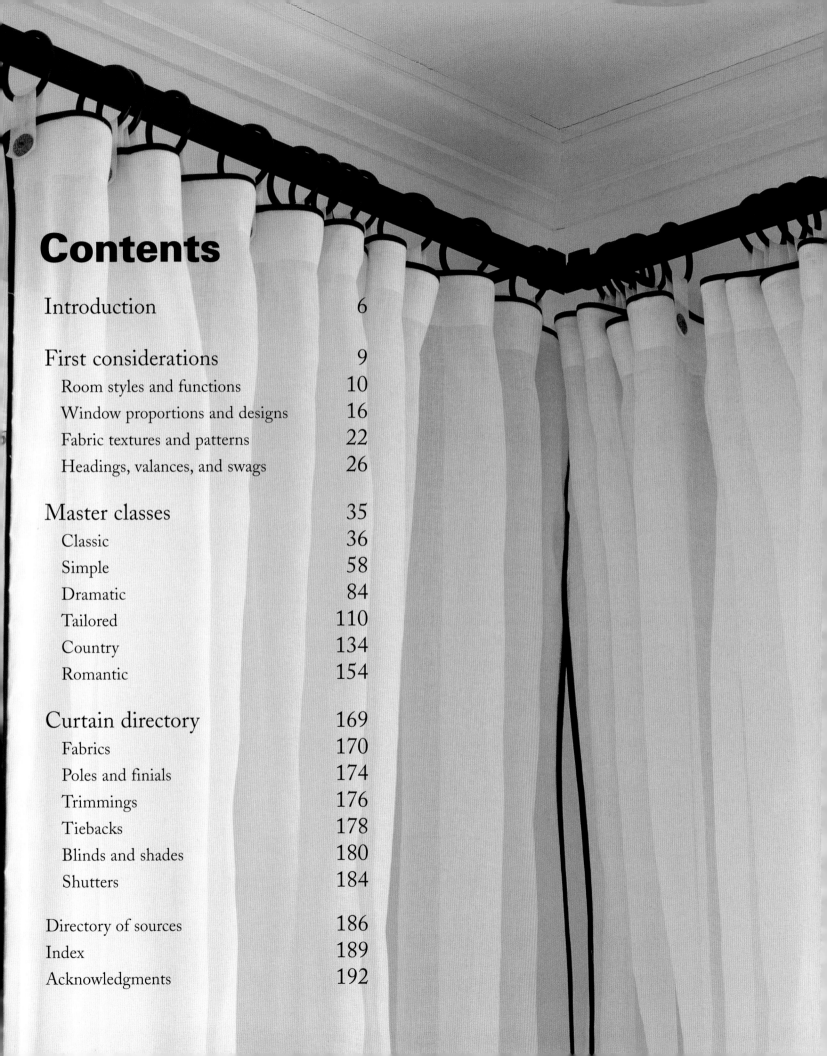

Contents

The need for a new set of curtains in my own apartment brought home to me how dramatically things have changed in the world of windows over the past decade. I became aware of a sea change that affected the style of window treatments more than almost any other area of decoration. It seemed time to completely readdress the whys and wherefores of drapes. There were new ways of making them, new fabrics, and new technologies. Here was a book aching to be written.

Talking to the talented designers who give master classes here on the art of curtains and drapes opened up the subject even further. Window treatments are simpler now; gone are flounces, chintzes, and the hard minimalist lines. The classic designers are looking for greater simplicity and the minimalists are looking for a softer edge.

A revolution in fabric technology means that it is no longer necessary to line and interline a curtain to protect delicate fabric or keep out drafts. It is possible to hang sheer silk at the window for privacy rather than a twitching nylon net; to weave metallic thread; trim lightweight silk with heavy velvet; and make curtains of suede and leather. And there have been notable changes to curtain hardware—hidden tracks, rivet headings, and boat fixtures allow new design ideas. Linings, toppers, and valances are no longer essential; simple layers and exquisite detailing have taken over. All the designers and curtain makers with whom I talked agreed that the art is in the detail, and a wealth of wonderful handmade braiding and trimmings are now available. Ten years ago, who would have imagined curtains of sheer linen edged with crystal droplets or tiebacks made of exotic jewelry? So much is now possible. We hope this book will help a new generation of curtain makers, designers, and homeowners to achieve their curtain ambitions.

Each designer has a different approach, but all agree on two vital points, namely, drapes must be appropriate to the room and they must be perfectly executed by an expert maker. With this in mind, I talked to four such highly-skilled  makers to tease the tricks of their trade out of them. In London, I spoke to Stuart Hands and Len Carter, who are both highly experienced in the traditional craft, and to Doreen Scott, who trained as a theatrical costumier and came to curtain making with no preconceived ideas. In South Africa, I tracked down Angela Swaine, who has applied her traditional approach to the requirements particular to sun-drenched, southern hemisphere living.

First considerations

"Every room needs to be approached differently, because every room has its own purpose, its own scale, its different types of windows offering different views. Some rooms scream for drapes, others for shutters." GINNY MAGHER

Room styles and functions

ABOVE
Nancy Braithwaite is not normally associated with valances, but for this client she has created a very simple, elegant Empire style that befits the room. She has used simple, draped valances to hide the gap between the top of the window and the ceiling.

The sooner the curtain maker gets involved in the design of a new or remodeled room, the better. Curtain makers have to hang the drapes, and they like to know as much as possible about the overall architecture of a room. For example, they want to see how much space there is above the window and how far the moldings project. This all helps them to plan—and a well-planned drape is a well-hung drape.

These days, the style of the house does not necessarily dictate the style of the curtains. Traditional Victorian houses, for instance, often have totally modern interiors, with shades or blinds at the windows, which can work very well. There is now total freedom to create whatever mood or style of interior you want. That said, the designers I talked to all had some general rules to keep in mind when thinking about the use to which various rooms of the house will be put.

RIGHT ABOVE
My previously blue-and-white kitchen has been given a radical new look with blinds of see-through "dishcloth" fabric that have stylish panels of beige suede in the center. It has completely changed my outlook, giving me more light and a wonderful view outside to the trees beyond.

FAR RIGHT ABOVE
Sera Hersham Loftus created for this client a sybaritic bedroom with antique lace at the window and a vintage black velvet curtain on the bed. A heavy linen Roman shade can be deployed to block out light.

RIGHT BELOW
A *portière* drape from Jacques Garcia hangs on a simple rod above the door. He has used an elaborate fabric with a decadent fringe to give this classic seventeenth-century hallway a theatrical touch of warmth.

FAR RIGHT BELOW
Sera Hersham Loftus's own bathroom proves that rules about simple, plain blinds or shades for bathrooms are made to be broken. She has draped her full-length windows with pink silk saris.

Frédéric Méchiche has given a novel slant to an exquisite French drawing room by using bamboo shades under his beautifully draped silk curtains. It's the contrast of textures, styles, and eras that makes this window treatment such a success.

Room by room

Living rooms are designed to impress, to show your lifestyle, and create a look that is individual. If you have a stunning view, you might not want to have any drapes at all, or you might want to use dress curtains in order to frame the view, add a dash of theatrical excitement, and take the hard edges off the window. However, if you are planning to do away with curtains, it is worth considering that at night, a dark window can look like a black hole, unless you have a specially designed lighting scheme either indoors or out. If your windows can be looked into from the outside, then the curtains should be functional, but they don't just provide privacy. Curtains can add warmth (especially if they have been lined and interlined). They also can be used to disguise poor architectural features or enhance good ones.

RIGHT ABOVE

A window flanked by French doors gets the architectural treatment from Vicente Wolf. He has painted the window frame black to capture the view, and added softness with simple columns of sheer fabric.

RIGHT BELOW

This bedroom by Emily Todhunter is relaxed and inviting. She has used two different weights of the same fabric, infusing the bedroom with light while guaranteeing privacy.

OPPOSITE

A very masculine media room by David Collins is visually separated from the garden room beyond by strong columns of fabric that have an inset stripe.

Nancy Braithwaite designed this luxuriously opulent four-poster bed, and hung it with beautifully lined, heavy curtains—in stark contrast to the minimal use of fabric at the window.

A Nancy Braithwaite bathroom is supplied with an architectural Roman blind in a shade of taupe that echoes the wood tones of the ceiling, and uses it again for the upholstered chair.

Sera Hersham Loftus's hallway needed some visual privacy, but not at the expense of natural light. She used a wonderful antique lace sheer, in keeping with the fabric lanterns and the elaborate ironwork on the stairs.

"Curtains have got to be user-friendly. Whatever the scheme, it must work practically."

ANGELA SWAINE

Bedrooms introduce major concerns of privacy and darkness. All the designers I talked to were in agreement that some clients will demand total blackout, and it's always a good idea to give children this option, so that they can get to sleep on light summer evenings. If curtains are lined with blackout material, you will always be in darkness when the curtains are drawn. For more flexibility, choose blackout blinds or under curtains with a separate, more translucent layer on top. Shutters also work really well for children, as long as they are easy to open and shut, because they let air through at night.

One of the curious anomalies that became apparent as I talked to the designers was that the more minimalist their tastes—for half-empty rooms and simple white roller blinds—the more outrageously they dressed their beds. All agreed that bed curtains should be generous and given as much height as possible. There are three ways of hanging them: from a coronet attached to the ceiling or the wall behind the bed; from a half-tester or tester,

a frame hung from the ceiling; or from the structure of a traditional four-poster bed.

Bathrooms and kitchens are places of steam, damp, and grease, which is not what curtains need. Bathrooms may be the place for etched glass panes or panels of mirror glass let into the windows. Kitchens don't need curtains swooping down into the sink, but simple panels, shutters, or easily cleaned wooden blinds can look cool and provide atmosphere. If you want curtains in the kitchen, keep the design simple and use a fabric such as mattress ticking.

Halls and corridors don't necessarily need curtains hung at the windows, but the general consensus amongst the designers was that there is no reason why you can't enjoy a drape just because it looks good. Curtains can add touches of color and comfort wherever needed. You can use tied back curtains or *portières*, which are curtains used over doors or instead of doors, to break up a long corridor or to curtain off a section of the hall, maybe for a dining area.

"Curtains can disguise a multitude of sins—they can make odd windows match, improve the proportions of an ordinary room, and enhance those of a lovely one." LEN CARTER

Window proportions and designs

ABOVE LEFT
A Palladian window, with its large, arched center panel, is beautiful but hard to dress, and often best left alone. Jacquelynne P. Lanham has drawn attention to the lovely proportions of this loft room window with a halo of plates.

ABOVE RIGHT
Bill Blass's exquisite home was blessed with beautifully proportioned Classic Revival windows. They have been left unadorned, the recessed shutters providing coverage when required.

The shape and type of a window will often suggest a particular treatment. My design gurus came up with the following window treatment rules—although they were also keen to point out that all rules are made to be broken.

Tall, narrow windows are the easiest to dress, because the exquisite proportions give a room height and grandeur. It is best to avoid over-dressing them and to concentrate on the vertical. When dealing with an arched window, it is advisable to ignore the arch, take the curtains up to the ceiling on either side, and avoid obscuring the line of the arch with a valance or shade. Alternatively, an arched window could be a good candidate for a free-standing screen instead of a fixed curtain treatment. Deep-set windows look good with shades or shutters over the window area and dress curtains to the side.

Bay windows are the most difficult of all to deal with, because you invariably need to have brackets holding up the track just where you don't want them. If the room is large, you can put curtains either side that will obliterate the bay when drawn. Otherwise, you have to hang heavy dress curtains either side and one or two sets of lighter drawing curtains within the bay, using the cornices or a valance to hide the fixings and tracks. The most glamorous solution is to have curtains that pull into the bay, but this is often not possible.

Other window shapes can also present initial problems. French doors that open inward need curtains that can stack on the wall either side. Generally, French doors look better without valances. Awkward windows, such as dormers, skylights, and clerestories (high rows of windows, such as those you might find in a converted church) are generally better off with custom-made shades.

RIGHT ABOVE
The bay window in my bedroom has under curtains of pashmina and over curtains of organza designed and made by Stuart Hands. The valance, which hides the track following the line of the bay, is made of two antique giltwood valance boards joined together and softened with a valance of pleated organza.

FAR RIGHT ABOVE
There are no visual tricks in this drawing room designed by Jacquelynne P. Lanham, just an elegant simplicity. The curtains on the full-length arched windows hang like pillars either side, leaving the lovely sweep of the glazed arches uncluttered.

RIGHT BELOW
Perihan Al-Uzri has dressed the gable end of this garden room with narrow blinds that follow the lines of the vertical glazing bars. It makes opening the door easy and practical, and filters the light.

FAR RIGHT BELOW
A bay window with attitude from Kit Kemp has a colorful and neat inverted pleat valance. The trim of feathers gives the window an exotic touch.

Measuring

Every measurement of a window and the wall needs to be taken, from ceiling to floor, from corner to corner. Then each needs taking again. You should never assume that two apparently identical windows are exactly the same; and it is important to always measure the exact profile of the moldings. You might want to take a photograph of the wall, so that you can study it at leisure, considering the window proportions and features before deciding on a treatment. In any case, curtains should hang from under the ceiling molding, or from the ceiling in a modern home, and all the way down to the floor. As far as I can gather, there are very few exceptions to this rule.

Each curtain will need a minimum of two times the width of the window, a maximum of three. The lighter the fabric, the more you will need. Far too many people make the mistake of skimping on fabric, so the curtains end up looking like fly screens. You've got to go that extra mile to match up the patterns properly and to bring the curtains to the floor and to the ceiling. Not one of the curtain makers with whom I talked had a kind word for short curtains or those that didn't quite make it to the floor. Be generous with the fabric for your curtains, invest in having them well-made and resist the temptation to be over elaborate—it is always easier to add than to take away. A useful tip when measuring up for your curtains is to be sure to allow for the thickness of a pole and all its fixings, if these are what you plan to use. Many people forget to take account of the size of the curtain hardware.

"Fabrics have a life of their own. Some of them want to float free, others will want to hang heavy—they'll tell you where they want to go."

DOREEN SCOTT

RIGHT
This is a detail of a curtain by Doreen Scott, made for my entrance hall. The generous layers are caught in scoops at different levels, which makes them look very glamorous. We gave the hall a completely new lease on life just by changing heavy under curtains for these *devoré* velvet sheers.

BELOW LEFT
A curtain is used as a room divider in an interior designed by Frédéric Méchiche. It is an opulent fall of heavy silk, lined and interlined, and breaking luxuriously on the floor.

BELOW RIGHT
Three layers of curtains hang in my drawing room in London. My brief to Doreen Scott was to make curtains that shimmered and were hardly there. The layers hang separately. Nearest the window is a layer of silk; then there's a layer of gossamer mohair; and on the inside, a panel of lace.

LEFT
In a sitting room by Kelly Hoppen, taupe curtains hang over iridescent sheers. They are attached to the pole with rings and ties of a darker hue, adding a degree of interest and drawing the eye upward.

BELOW
These signature curtains by Coorengel and Calvagrac hang in a drawing room overlooking the rooftops of Paris. The key-pattern braid gives a sharp edge to the glorious sweep of deep eggplant-colored silk. The black pole disappears visually into the wall, so there's no distracting fuss at ceiling level.

Anatomy of a good curtain

Good curtains are an investment that should enhance the design and proportions of the windows and become part of the architecture of the room. The best curtains are handmade in every detail, apart from the seams joining the widths. Good curtain makers do not use heading tapes, but create every pleat, gather, and hem by hand. With a machine you always get a little pulling, so a handmade curtain will always hang better, no matter what fabric is used, be it sackcloth or silk. If your curtains are designed to last for twenty-five years, they will certainly need to be lined—and interlined—to protect the outer,

"Dress curtains should always have a finished leading edge and base, a reverse side as good as the face, and should preferably be lined and interlined to give them weight."

STUART HANDS

RIGHT

To emphasize the height of this room, Nancy Braithwaite has used a bold stripe to take the eye up to the ceiling. She hung the curtains from a simple pole with a track hidden inside it. The horizontal lines of the bench anchor the verticality of the curtains.

BELOW

Eldo Netto has used an amazing black, white, and gray animal-print fabric for these curtains and teamed them with shades in subtle natural shades of taupe and cream. The effect is an unexpected interpretation of elegance.

decorative fabric. Of course, not many people want their curtains to last that long, and these days unlined curtains are popular because they are lighter, cheaper, and more versatile.

A regular curtain is made by first machining the widths together, then lock-stitching the interlining to the main fabric. Then the hems are sewn using herringbone stitching that allows for a little "give" and the lining is attached using an invisible stitching technique. Next come the headings. Buckram is inserted to stiffen the heading, which is then sewn by hand. Finally, the hooks are sewn on, also by hand. So it is hardly surprising that good curtains are expensive.

If you can't afford new curtains, there are a number of things that can be done to give your windows a facelift. A new border of contrasting fabric stitched to the leading edge and base of a curtain will frame a window in a whole new way. The addition of a voile, colored or plain, on a separate track or pole, could change the whole atmosphere of the room. To give a plain shade a new lease on life, a small panel of gorgeously expensive fabric can be appliquéd down the center.

> "I use texture rather than pattern. I've started making suede curtains, which look and feel absolutely amazing. I think the feel of the fabric is terribly important, which is why we do a lot of pashminas and cashmeres."
>
> BERNIE DE LE CUONA

Fabric textures and patterns

On pages 170 through 173, we have gathered together a tiny sample, some of our favorites, from the massive choice of available fabrics, which is extending all the time. While the choice is vast, the rule dictating choice and quantity is quite simple—to be generous. Curtains that look skimpy, even if made from expensive fabric, will never look as good as generous curtains made from cheap fabric.

Curtains are about fashion and there's no reason why you can't use *devoré* velvet, beaded lace, wool suiting, pashmina, PVC, or black leather. The distinctions between dress-weight fabrics and furnishing fabrics have virtually disappeared, and many of the most exquisite curtains are made from dress-weight silk and linen. The advantage of choosing furnishing fabrics, however, is that they are made on wider looms—up to 10 feet (3 meters)—while dress-weights can be as narrow as 28 in (72 cm). If you fall in love with an expensive but narrow fabric, consider using one width of it as a panel or border on a background of something less expensive but more robust.

A good piece of advice before you commit to a fabric is to buy a large, returnable sample. When you get home, throw it over a pole, and live with it for a week or so. It is amazing how the sheen, color, and texture of a fabric responds differently to sunlight and showers, morning light and evening light. You can't make an informed choice from a quick flick through a sample book.

Most of the curtain makers favored plain, natural fabrics, because they retained their freshness and coordinated with any kind of look. The most quoted favorite fabric was linen, followed by silk taffeta. Textured silk, ticking, and cotton damask also fell into the easy-to-work-with department. Silk damask apparently has a life of its own and velvet and very fine crêpe de Chine are very, very difficult to get right. For complex designs, the consensus of opinion is to use either plain fabrics or tiny patterns and rely on trims, borders, and contrasting linings to emphasize the design. Conversely, if you have chosen an elaborate fabric, such as chintz or toile de Jouy, opt for a simple design.

The number of synthetics that have become available in the last ten years or so has revolutionized the working life of every curtain maker. Not so long ago, polyester was a dirty word, but now everyone has embraced modern fibers and is working with fabrics such as fake suedes and metallic threads, which produce the most amazing effects.

Gone are the days of yellowing net curtains, but everyone was in agreement that nets did serve a purpose—they let in light and protected privacy. Today's sheer voile and cheesecloth do much the same thing, but with a pizzazz that makes them a vital component of the twenty-first-century look. Translucent fabrics range from the thinnest silk organza to optical fabrics that change with the light. They hold shapes that would have been impossible twenty years ago. Now you can play with shadows and diffuse light through gossamer-thin fabrics, which have a strength of tensile steel.

FAR LEFT
A woven striped sheer catches the light and plays with it, giving a room a wonderful luminous quality.

RIGHT ABOVE
In a room with a view designed by Nancy Braithwaite, the wall of windows has floor-to-ceiling gauze shades to soften the sunlight without detracting from the view.

FAR RIGHT ABOVE
My gray flannel curtains by Stuart Hands kick over any sober associations with their luxurious crumpled lining and trimming of crystal beads on the leading edge. The lining fabric is contour linen woven with a dissolvable thread. When washed, the subsequent shrinkage causes the stunning crumpled effect.

RIGHT BELOW
A very modern take on the pattern-on-pattern look is Kit Kemp's patchwork curtains of nineteenth-century French quilts.

FAR RIGHT BELOW
Cutting edge curtains from David Collins are made from a patchwork of suede cut so the nap of the fabric catches the light at different angles. They are pulled across using bamboo poles so that they are not constantly handled.

TOP LEFT
Two layers of curtains hang perfectly to the floor. The filmy inner sheer is sewn with tiny diamanté beads, and the heavy amethyst silk outer curtains are weighted and pleated in contrast.

ABOVE LEFT
My dramatic hall curtains have two separate layers, but it is only the inner layer that is drawn when I want to transform the hall into a dining room. The antique giltwood valance board hides both the tracks and the headings.

ABOVE RIGHT
Suzy Clé designed this bedroom for her younger daughter, who wanted something bold and modern. She got these bold black-and-white striped curtains, stunningly juxtaposed with feather printed shades in a terra-cotta color.

Linings and layers

Fifteen years ago, curtains were always lined and interlined, but today unlined curtains are very fashionable. The trend is toward using far greater quantities of fabric in the width, giving plenty of generosity and fullness, and to work with several layers, usually two but often three. All the layers work independently on different tracks, so you can vary the fabrics that you see by drawing one or other across the window. The fabrics chosen may vary in texture, from heavyweight dress drapes to the sheerest inner curtains; or in color. The strongest color is usually on the outside, shading toward a paler inner layer.

Many people who like their curtains lined pay close attention to the lining fabric. They may choose a check or stripe as a contrast to the main fabric, which looks good glimpsed on fold-backs from within and is particularly attractive when viewed from the outside of the house.

RIGHT
A typical look from Mimmi O'Connell, in which she has teamed a filmy sheer with a bold black fabric. The border of self-colored embroidery softens the impact as it catches the light.

Headings, valances, and swags

The type of heading, and of valance if one is used, from which a curtain is hung dictates the whole appearance of the window treatment. It is important to use the right heading for the right fabric. It would be no good, for example, having a wonderful fabric with a large pattern if the heading scrunches it up so much that the pattern can't be appreciated. Similarly, valances are often dramatic additions, setting the style of a window treatment, and they need to be chosen to complement the fabric and the overall style. The beauty of it all is that there are so many fantastic heading and valance options to choose from.

RIGHT
A slot-headed silk dress curtain, made for me by Stuart Hands, is not designed to be drawn, so this type of heading is ideal. The wide pole is finished off with gorgeous gilded finials.

RIGHT ABOVE
Striped off-the-peg sheers from Blanc d'Ivoire hang as almost flat panels from a simple rod. They are casually tied to the rings with ribbons made from the same sheer fabric, creating a valance-like effect at the top.

FAR RIGHT ABOVE
A sitting room by Kit Kemp displays two colorways of striped silk sewn together in panels and threaded onto a pole through metal rings set into the fabric. The pointed pleats decorating the top of the curtains act as an informal valance design.

RIGHT BELOW
Perihan Al-Uzri has carefully draped silk over a pole to frame a bedroom window. The fabric is tied back into bunches and allowed to puddle luxuriously onto the floor. It is a very Empire look, but not in the least old-fashioned.

FAR RIGHT BELOW
Suzy Clé created these curtains for her elder daughter, who has ambitions to be an opera set designer. The soft, sheer fabric has been gathered into a smocked heading and dotted with pretty little rosettes.

ABOVE

In two coordinating layers of drapes from Mimmi O'Connell, the ties that attach the outer curtain match the edging and the under curtains. Loose ribbons finish off the tops of the curtain splendidly. It's an informal look, best suited to fabrics such as plain or striped ticking, linens, and cottons.

LEFT

A new take on rod and rings is this system of inserting the rings into the fabric and threading the rod directly through. It is called a rivet heading, and is best for curtains that are not often drawn.

Headings

The rule of thumb is to use simple headings wherever possible, but especially on elaborate fabrics. The easiest heading, that suits practically every style and fabric, is the traditional French pleat. Goblet pleats are dramatic and, accordingly, should never be less than 6 in (15 cm) tall. Pencil pleats must be created by hand in order to look good, and this could turn out to be expensive. Gathered headings suit informal curtains. Slot headings conceal the pole from which the curtains hang, so the drapes don't really draw that well. This makes them good for sheers and cheesecloth, but not for anything too heavy. Smocked headings are very decorative and best for plain silk or simple stripes; and looped or tie headings are usually used for informal curtains hanging from a simple pole.

"The French heading is classic and it is the easiest to use. It can be used on a pole, on a track, on a fascia board, whether beneath a valance or not. It takes only a narrow space when pulled apart and hangs well, both simply and with tiebacks."

STUART HANDS

1 French heading on rings and pole. This is by far the easiest heading to use because it is so versatile. It bunches up well, the curtains filling only a narrow space when pulled aside, and can be used on virtually any fabric.

2 Tab heading. This neat system consists of tabs with fastenings that are pushed through the fabric. It is suitable for heavier, preferably plain, fabrics.

3 Tie heading. Unlined lace panels are tied on with silk velvet ribbon and unlined mohair outer curtains are attached with pearl buttons over a pole. The effect illustrates the new, free-flowing style of today's curtains.

4 Smocked heading. Smocking is difficult to create and extremely rich in detail, and is therefore not to be hidden. This is a heading style that could be used on a shorter window. Use plain fabric or one with a small pattern—never a large design.

5 Cape heading. So called because the curtain fabric—matching or contrasting—is turned over on itself to form a loose cape that falls over the heading, preferably a simple gather or a French pleat. It is a very effective country look.

6 A French heading on a track is attached to a fascia board and covered in fabric to hide the track and shade fixings. It looks neat and well finished.

7 Gathered heading. This looks great with stripes and checks, because it changes the emphasis of the pattern at the top. For this reason, it is not really suitable for large, repeat patterns.

8 A modern ring-and-clip system. The fabric is held in pleats by the clips, giving the pleats a precision that is best suited to plain fabrics with a little weight to them, such as burlap or heavy linen.

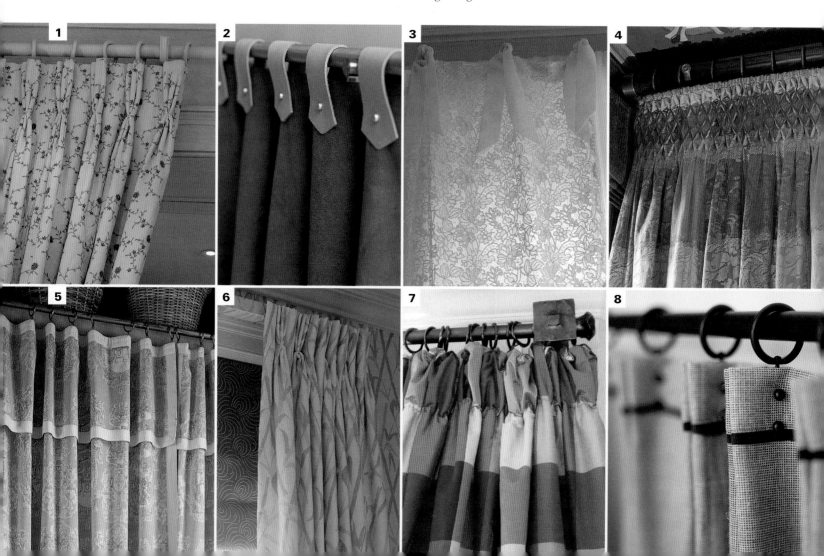

9   9 Rivet-headed curtain. A modern look, it is best suited to canvas or other stiff fabric. The under curtains are on a separate, thinner rod and tied to simple rings.

10 Detail of a robust rivet-headed curtain. This is an excellent way of dealing with fabrics such as thick felt, synthetic suede, or leather, because it does not require the fabric to be pleated.

11 Simple roll-up shade fixing. The lightweight shade is hung on wall-mounted rosettes. The bold key-pattern braid both stiffens and decorates the top of the shades.

12 Pencil pleat heading. This is made up of very fine, precise pleats stacked together and it works on valances as well. A very versatile heading that looks good with fabrics that catch the light, such as silks and satins.

13 Slot heading. The pole is slotted through a pocket sewn in the fabric. It is a very elegant heading for dress curtains that do not draw, but fasten with tiebacks or Italian stringing (as used for theater curtains).

14 A tie heading with contrasting ribbons. This type of heading is ideal for floating, filmy fabrics, such as sheers. It is well suited to thin iron poles and metal rings.

15 Inverted pleat heading. A very simple heading that looks good when drawn, as it tends to bunch up rather clumsily when pulled back. Gives a sleek modern look and an opportunity to play with large repeat patterns.

16 Goblet pleat heading. A classic style that is perfect for showing off larger patterns. The goblets themselves are usually filled with wadding to hold their shape.

1 A soft, shaped valance in the formal American Country House style. If you are going for a fancy valance shape, trim it boldly so the shape speaks for itself.

2 A swagged valance. The swags —hanging pleats—have to be carefully arranged from a fabric heavy enough to hold the shape.

3 A simple gathered heading topped off with an antique giltwood valance board. It's the classic way with a valance and the modern way with fabric that makes this treatment so successful.

4 Hard, shaped valances give these tall windows an elegant flourish. With ceilings this high, flamboyance works perfectly.

5 Pretty, shaped scalloped valance that is, in fact, very simple. It's the fabric and the border that attract the attention, rather than any fancy pleating methods.

6 Hard valance stiffened with buckram into a slightly bowed shape, conceived as part of the architecture of the room. The strong, straight lines of this type of valance are perfect with curtains that hang straight, unfastened by tiebacks.

7

8

9

10

11

7 Pointed cape valance made in the same way as one with the curtain fabric flapped over the top. The points are tipped with tiny beads for added pizzazz.
8 Traditional swagged valances look wonderful with traditional curtains. There's a lovely rhythm to the restrained lines of the swag and the tiebacks.
9 A valance that's not really a valance at all. It's a swag of fringed fabric thrown across the top of these curtains like a Flamenco dancer's shawl.
10 A pretty gathered valance is trimmed with fine silk rope. It works perfectly with the full gathered curtains in a romantic and feminine bedroom.
11 Another example of the dramatic shawl valance, cutting a dash over inverted pleat curtains in an arrangement that is not to be disturbed.

Valances and swags

Valances are an acquired taste, and opinions amongst our designers were divided. They hide a multitude of sins and can make an extremely tall window more intimate, by visually drawing it down. Yet valances cut out light, and if you are using a patterned fabric, the complications mount as you relate the design of the valance to that of the fabric.

There are basically four types of valance. Hard valances are made of wood covered in fabric. Flat valances are made of fabric, sometimes lined with buckram, and may be box-pleated, but not gathered. Fabric valances may be softly gathered, ruched, or pencil-pleated; and lambrequins are stiff, shaped panels, arched in the middle, which may or may not be covered in fabric. Valances should never be shorter in depth than 20 in (50 cm), or they will appear out of proportion. Equally, they should not obscure the tops of the windows, because the best quality of light comes from above.

Swag draperies, with their carefully arranged folds, are generally seen today as a totally unnecessary complication that is less than fashionable. The effect can be quite striking if handled well, but it must be remembered that swags are essentially Victorian and Edwardian in style, and certainly not eighteenth-century, as many people would have you believe. Authentic eighteenth-century and early nineteenth-century curtains were actually quite sparing with fabric, and often thrown nonchalantly over a pole, as we might do today.

When interviewing the designers featured here, I was struck by their sheer professionalism. They are specialists who really know and understand their craft and have the generosity of spirit to share their experience with us.

There are as many opinions as there are interviews, but on one point all agreed—the old rules no longer apply. Because almost anything is now possible, the choices are overwhelming, and I am glad to be able to present some guidance.

I have divided the master classes into six categories, but many of the designers can and do produce work in any or all of them. After all, a good designer can create a home of his or her client's dreams, in whatever style.

Master classes

Classic curtain design pays some considerable homage to legendary figures from the world of interior decoration. In particular, it owes a huge debt to the late John Fowler, co-founder in 1933 of the British partnership of Colefax & Fowler. Inspired by his rigorously classical decorative arts education, Fowler defined the English country house look of grand, lived–in chic with an emphasis on comfort. This became a style that traveled the world taking on many different guises. The designers featured in these master classes all spring from this glorious tradition. They share a huge depth of knowledge and a magnificent sense of style; and all have had their expertise stretched to the limits when solving design problems such as lack of architectural symmetry or an unattractive view. This does not mean that classically trained designers always produce classic work—far from it. These designers achieve superb results in many different styles, but they always work from their fund of immense experience and knowledge.

In defining classic style, words such as "grace" and "symmetry" come to mind to describe a look that works best in rooms of grand and gracious proportions. It is a style that requires space, because it is strong on color, generous with fabric, and clever in its use of pattern-on-pattern. If you are going to "do" classic, then it has to be done well. The 1980s saw a deplorable rash of "country house" interiors with draped and swagged, over elaborate curtains crammed into the tiny, knocked-through downstairs rooms of urban townhouses. The result was a backlash against a style that, in fact, still has much to offer.

Like all lasting traditions, the classic style has changed, adapted for a place in the twenty-first century. Designers today may use plain fabrics or simple stripes instead of damask and velvet, but their curtains are still beautifully made, draped, and weighted—they are still essays in perfection. Even if your taste does not run to silks and taffetas or to antiques and chandeliers, I urge you to browse through the classics and enjoy the expertise and style on display.

Classic

ELDO NETTO

In 1978, Eldo Netto exchanged a
career in international banking for
one in textile design. He acquired
the vestiges of an old New York
company called Cowtan & Tout and
over the next ten years reestablished
it as the definitive purveyor of
high-quality, multi-colored chintzes.
Intending to retire, he sold the
company in 1992—but soon came
back into design with his new
business, Travers, developing prints
and wallcoverings in traditional
and classical style. Travers is now
developing beautiful fabrics that are
affordable, without compromising
on quality.

❝ During the 1980s, curtains achieved their most elaborate
expression. Top-of-the-range decorators surpassed themselves—if
curtains were worth doing, they were worth doing to excess. At this
time, so much money was channeled into upholstery, elaborate
drapes, and all sorts of cosmetic accessories that people were forced
to compromise on function and structure. We've all attempted to shift
gears over the last several years, and the look now is much more
linear and pared down, with more emphasis on the architectural and
much less on complicated fabric treatments.

There was a tendency in the 1980s to pile one
print on top of another, but that complicated
interplay between patterns and prints looks
old-fashioned now. There's a new sobriety in
the way people want their rooms to look.
Prints now often play a less important role,
while textures and plain fabrics have become
more important—especially linens and linen
blends—and the palette is more neutral than
in the past. The way we ornament our surroundings is influenced by this new simplicity.

Trimmings, however, have held their
sway, because with the advent of simpler
fabrics, a lot of people feel curtain treatments
look naked without the detail of a wonderful
silk tassel or beaded trim. So, paradoxically,
elaborate trimmings continue to be an
important factor in window treatments.

MY OWN CURTAINS

I'm in the process of moving out of a penthouse and into a new apartment. The dining

OPPOSITE AND ABOVE
In the light and elegant drawing
room of his New York apartment,
Eldo Netto has used an almost
chiaroscuro fabric with a pattern
of animals. It is printed onto the
vertical yarns before the weft yarns
are added to the weave, giving the
silk the "'watered" look
characteristic of this process. The
pure silk curtains hang straight
from rings and poles finished in
a pewter tone.

room, which faced a brick wall, had a somewhat theatrical window treatment of yellow-and-white striped silk with warp-printed, floral bouquets. I've brought that over to the dining room of my new apartment, because it works, but in the living room I've installed simple draperies. They are straight down polyester stripes, as the room is exposed to very strong southern sun, but as they look like silk, the choice of polyester involved no compromise. My son, whose approach to architecture and design is more cutting edge than mine, suggested plain *café au lait*-colored silk with detailed edging. I'm happy with that. I'm reluctant to go the whole hog and risk having people say, "Migod, what gorgeous curtains," when what I really wanted them to notice was the room in its entirety.

CITY AND COUNTRY

I would say that elaborate valances and draperies have had their day as far as most city apartments are concerned, primarily because the lower ceilings in modern homes militate against fancy window treatments. In period houses, on the other hand, the picture can change. The amply scaled rooms with high ceilings that one finds in mansions in the South, for example, can accommodate the most luxurious drapes and valances. As we sell fabrics throughout the country, we must be attuned to different needs for different markets. While we do not make as many glazed chintzes as we used to, we continue to keep a good number on hand for clients who still want what has now become rather hard to find. For those looking for more "fashionable" options, we in the industry have geared up to provide unglazed chintz patterns printed on linen/cotton grounds and these much sought-after reinterpretations of the traditional fabrics can now be found in all the design centers.

Without minimizing the importance of plain and textured fabrics— silks, linens, and blends—it is interesting to note that the most successful fabric I have introduced in the last two decades is a

ABOVE RIGHT
In a master bedroom, curtains of hand-embroidered crewelwork from India are lined and edged with rose red silk. Privacy is ensured with a wooden slatted blind, and a Roman shade of plaid silk keeps out the light. This is a room of immense flair and finish.

ABOVE FAR RIGHT
In another bedroom, a detail of the gloriously faded-looking moiré striped curtains shows their colored bobble edging. Drapes such as these, made of a beautiful fabric, perfectly hung and wittily trimmed, epitomize the new way forward for the classic look.

BELOW RIGHT
The crewelwork curtains hang simply from gilded rings on a magnificent, antique, carved gilt pole with eccentric finials, which Eldo Netto takes with him whenever he moves homes. It gives great éclat to the room.

BELOW FAR RIGHT
Another antique gilded pole is used for the bobble edged curtains alongside the stylish counterpoint of an elaborate gilded picture frame. The dress curtains are invisibly held aside with the type of rip-cord used for theater curtains.

multi-colored print, twenty-five colors in all, in the form of a traditional floral bouquet. The fine linen background cloth is elegant, while at the same time sturdy and long-wearing. So, while the trend today may suggest that color plays only a limited role, my feeling is that what most clients are looking for are rooms that are not only comfortable and easy to live in and with, but ones that are pleasing to the eye—even "pretty." Achieving this can be quite daunting if your palette is confined to cream and beige with touches of puce. The simple look works best in sophisticated installations with a good deal of emphasis on serious art on the walls, but most of us do not find ourselves confronted with that particular challenge. Rather, I think that most people are drawn to what is perceived as a traditional approach to decorating. They like to start with an appealing, if not ravishing, fabric design and build a room around it. The window is the most fortuitous place to have that fabric —the place of honor, and therefore the logical starting point.

A DESIGN PHILOSOPHY

Fabrics are sensitive to light and heat. An unlined curtain will eventually rot if exposed to strong sunlight, even for relatively short periods. I wouldn't use an expensive fabric at a window without lining it, but manufacturers in India are now making a wide variety of silks of high quality at competitive prices, so that light can now be allowed to filter through a flutter of unlined curtains. Unlined curtains can look marvelous. My inclination would be to go for either the unlined look or the fully lined and interlined alternative. Anything in between smacks of compromise. As for having no curtains, blinds, or shades at all, well, I don't think most of us feel comfortable with the "fish-bowl" effect.

I'm not a decorator. Ideas for fabric designs are presented to me and I decide—together with my design director—whether we want to put that design into production. Our chief criterion is whether or not we like it. Our taste is quite classic, and the most important factor is color. The design is secondary. Color affects the way you feel, and if you're going to spend a lot of time in a room, you've got to feel right within it. I love red and green and all their variations, whether in textures, stripes, or prints.

I think a reluctance to be open-minded is a mistake—to reject a new idea without considering it. Some people might think they know what they like, but have never considered the possibilities of using colors such as lavender or chartreuse, and they'll stick to the predictable. That's a sin of omission. And the sin of commission is to make rooms you can't live in. 99

Our chief criterion is whether we like a design or not. Our taste is quite classic, and the most important factor is color—the design is secondary

Eldo Netto

JACQUES GARCIA

An early training in applied arts, a passion for conceptual art, and a collection of seventeenth-century French furniture equipped Jacques Garcia for his later transformations of period interiors. His large-scale visions of elegance and richness have been realized in stunning buildings throughout France, including opulent hotels and private homes. His creativity and visual flair have even been put to good use by national museums. For example, in 1993 he designed an exhibition about Marie Antoinette at the Museé Carnavalet. He now travels the world as an interior decorator.

66 When I was a child, my father, who was passionate about architecture and the decorative arts, took me to visit Champ de Bataille, a château in Normandy, a perfect example of the seventeenth-century baroque style. I bought the château in 1992. I knew I wanted to acquire it to showcase a collection of furniture and of royal objects from the seventeenth and eighteenth centuries—it was a perfect setting for them.

A HISTORICAL PERSPECTIVE

I brought my personal vision to the restoration of the château, which evokes an eighteenth-century notion of the pleasures of life. The result is not a historical museum, but a contemporary vision of a French Classic interior. My interiors have a historical foundation, but I develop something that can only be modern—we can never ignore our own century.

In the context of the decorative arts, the eighteenth century is associated with a period of seismic change in interior decoration. It was a period that reveled in a love of harmony and symmetry and a whole new concept of furnishings designed to relate to each other. Window drapes became distinct from wall hangings, and they were usually single, made of fairly transparent silk, taffeta, or linen and hung by metal rings on metallic rods. Come to think of it, that is a very contemporary look.

I use a lot of fabrics: curtains, throws, tablecloths, pillows, upholstery, tapestries; and I use everything from sumptuous damasks to cotton toile. For instance, in my *salon* in the private apartments at Champ de Bataille, the walls are covered with a simple

ABOVE LEFT

An opulent *portière* curtain between an entrance and a corridor in Jacques Garcia's grand Normandy château shows great use of red and gold. It has a trim of gold braid all around it, in keeping with the gilded woodwork of the château's interior.

ABOVE CENTER

In a corner of this room, Garcia has installed a shocking pink sheer festoon blind, adding an outrageous touch of modernity to the sea of red.

ABOVE RIGHT

A traditional Empire style tailored bed curtain in red silk damask matches the scalloped upholstered bed. The red and gold is used in a typically dramatic way, with a whimsical touch in the knots of fabric at the corners.

RIGHT

The small, antique copper bathtub would be lost in this formal, masculine environment were it not for the eye-catching scalloped canopy of raspberry-and-cream French toile, with a washable lining of soft muslin. It is a flamboyant and amusing touch.

calico, which contrasts with the luxurious velvet in the other rooms. The floor coverings are of natural fibers and the simple drapes are in keeping with the walls. The effect is that of a country house. It's not possible to treat drapes separately from the rest. I don't think you can walk into a fabric showroom and just choose a fabric—you've got to have the atmosphere you want to create completely clear in your mind before you make that decision.

INTERIOR HARMONY

The design starting point is a space defined by a solid foundation of harmony and symmetry. Windows are an integral part of this concept. If, for one reason or another, harmony is lacking in an interior, a well thought-out window treatment can hide a multitude of architectural flaws. Once a space has been defined, I add neoclassic and Oriental touches of fantasy, indulgence and comfort, together with French classic references and hints of modernism. I like to think that my work creates a first impression of coherence, but that on closer inspection you become aware of the mix of styles. 99

ABOVE

Curtains of striped yellow and gray silk match the colorway of the leaf design wallpaper, giving the walls of this small, high-ceilinged bedroom a sense of unity. A burgundy silk valance matches the depth of the deep faux ebony cornice and the line of the drapery gathered on a half-tester above the bed.

In the eighteenth century, window drapes became distinct from wall hangings, and they were usually single, made of fairly transparent silk, taffeta, or linen and hung by metal rings on metallic rods

Jacques Garcia

NINA CAMPBELL

Nina Campbell's decorating career began when she worked as assistant to John Fowler of the prestigious design company Colefax & Fowler. For thirty years she has occupied a place as one of Great Britain's leading interior designers. Her love for the tools of her trade led her to design her own ranges of fabrics and wallpapers for Osborne & Little, as well as carpets, rugs, and paints for a range of companies. In 2001, she opened Nina Campbell at Bridge Studios in London, which offers a wide range of decorating materials and acts as an invaluable resource center for interior decorators.

A pink-and-white room in a typical English classic style. The patterns and colors of the wallpaper and soft furnishings all relate to one another, and the curtains pull the whole scheme together. The softly gathered, frilled valances and the bobble trim are all part of the pretty, feminine detailing. The plain white silk curtains emphasize the light that floods into the room and sound a note of calm in a sea of detailed prints.

> 66 I was trained in the English Country House decorating tradition by the founding father, John Fowler. He worked mainly in large houses, and everyone thinks his clients had money to burn, but they didn't. One of the things John Fowler taught me was not to throw everything out and start again, but to reuse what was good.

The curtains Nina chose for the drawing room of her Chelsea, London home represent the way her style has evolved and become simpler and sharper over the years. These generous but unfussy cream silk curtains pool gently onto a stripped and polished wood floor.

A detail of gray silk curtains elsewhere in the house shows tiebacks of silk rope trimmed with antique crystal tassels. Crystal has emerged in the twenty-first century as a very fashionable trimming. The look is one of cool and calm, but it remains intrinsically classic in style.

If a wonderful curtain had faded on the outside edge, then Fowler would take some velvet, dye it to get that patchy, worn look and make an eight-inch border for the leading edge and the base. I used that trick just the other day, because the fabric we wanted to replace had been discontinued. John Fowler's particular genius was in understanding that rooms had to be comfortable. He'd work wonders using pattern and texture and adding exquisite doses of color for tablecloths, the odd chair, or pillow.

CYCLES OF EXCESS
Fifteen to twenty years ago, people insisted on having valances, swags, and drapes even on picture windows in low-ceilinged rooms.

That completely destroyed the true market for the grand curtain, which only looks right on a grand window. Festoon blinds, swags, and drapes belong at beautifully proportioned large windows, not in bathrooms, but it's amazing how some people still can't see that. It's like someone small wanting a dress she's seen on a six-foot model and imagining she'll look just the same. It will never work. Curtains are an investment; they are expensive. If you have to make a compromise, I'd rather have a good curtain maker and a less expensive fabric.

Luckily, people are becoming more aware of architecture now, and aware of the need for light in a room; they have generally moved on from the excesses of the 1980s. Taste is cyclical. Elsie de Woolf came along in 1904 and swept away the excesses of the Victorian era, when they had up to seven pairs of heavy drapes at one window. She brought in the idea of light, English floral chintzes and plain curtains—but the chintz look then became overdone. The minimalists have swept that away for us this time around, but the good chintzes will survive, just as the good velvets, brocades, and chenilles so beloved by the Victorians have done.

PLAINS AND PATTERNS

I get very excited about fabrics, especially about the way they hang. I remember doing a room with five thirty-foot-high windows. That's a lot of fabric to get wrong! We designed grand and wonderful swags and chose an unusual wool satin in a glorious yellow. The fabric hangs beautifully, has a flat look to it, and a slightly woven texture. A pattern would have looked ridiculous and a shiny fabric would have looked awful. As it was, the daughter of the house walked into the room and didn't even notice the curtains, because they blended with their surroundings. I think that's very important. You can get pattern and excitement from pillows and upholstery, but I think the expanse of curtain fabric needs to be more restful. When I do use patterns, I use walling to match. I once did a bedroom in a wonderful rose pattern, and the client said she felt as if she'd fallen into a bed of roses.

ABOVE

This is the traditional classic window treatment, personified with a swagged and tailed valance, fringing to draw the eye to the line of the drape, and color-coordinated silk dress curtains, lined and interlined to hang perfectly. It looks wonderful in a high-ceilinged period room.

LEFT

A stately hall demands a stately treatment, and this one has glorious red curtains to add warmth and to balance the impact of the staircase. The deep, traditional valance is fringed and corded, and the low tiebacks give the curtains a strong, simple line, like pillars.

The classic style is all about attention to detail. Generous swathes of ocher-colored curtaining hang against tobacco-colored walls, and carefully chosen silk ropes and braids define and finish to perfection.

A traditional, dramatic dress curtain framing a French window is designed to be held up and away from the opening doors, leaving the sunlight free to come streaming in to illuminate this busy study.

A FEEL FOR FABRIC

I love the feel of fabrics: damask, velvet, chenille, and printed linen. I also love floaty fabrics that let the light come through, such as sheer linen or silk taffeta, which I often use unlined. I would say the most exciting developments have come in the wonderful blends you get now. There's a linen-and-viscose mix with an interesting texture and a silk-and-cotton mix that has "body." I get very excited

about trimmings; there's such a variety of new stuff and a revival of things not seen since the eighteenth century, such as marabou balls, leather, and crystal beads.

We produce our own range of fabrics, and inspiration for the designs comes from all over the place—from visits to botanical gardens to old kimonos and main street fashion. This year we're concentrating on wisteria, hydrangeas, and roses. I'm having some wonderful silks made up in India and I think we're going to see chintz as in the original meaning of the word—the glaze on the surface of the fabric, not the floral patterns. 99

You can get pattern and excitement from pillows and upholstery, but the expanse of curtain fabric needs to be more restful. When I do use pattern, I use walling to match

Nina Campbell

JOHN STEFANIDIS

Born in Egypt and educated at
Oxford, England, John Stefanidis
started his London-based interior
design practice in 1967. His
extensive portfolio of work includes
the homes of clients in the UK,
USA, the Caribbean, France,
Switzerland, Italy, and Greece, and
illustrates work in homes in city and
country and both large and small.
His attention to the use of light and
color, and to the choice of fabrics
and the placement of furniture
within a space, have resulted in
interior design schemes that are
noted for their combinations of
style and practicality.

RIGHT ABOVE
A traditional, grand room of good proportions is
an ideal showcase for John Stefanidis' distinctive
style. Stunning blue-and-gilt walls almost steal
the show, but the generous curtains of unlined
eau de nil silk provide another grand element.

RIGHT BELOW
Green damask curtains against ocher walls make
for tonal harmony in this calming sitting room.
The curtains emphasize the vertical in this
high-ceilinged room, hanging straight from
inverted-pleat valances at ceiling height.

OPPOSITE
An elegant, beautifully proportioned room has
curtains that blend with the walls while retaining
a measure of surprise. Straight and plain, they
are edged with a bobble trim. The eye-catching
pleated swag valances are in a striped fabric to
match the walls.

❝ My philosophy is very simple. I advise clients to have as few
curtains as possible. Some rooms need them and others patently do
not. And just as you can't take one solution and apply it to a whole
house, you cannot take one idea and apply it to every window in the
same room. French doors that open inward dictate the kind of
treatment you might have.

We avoid floor-length curtains if the glass
does not go to the ground—but there are
exceptions. Some windows demand roller
blinds, which can vary from the very elaborate and luxurious to the simple—sometimes
unlined and often with cords and tassels in
colors to match or contrast.

FITNESS FOR PURPOSE
Wooden blinds (once known as *jalousies*) are
a most effective solution, particularly in hot
climates where the light can be blinding. If
shutters are on the outside, a thin curtain can
cut the light—the simpler the better. If there
are no exterior shutters, louvers control light
most satisfactorily indoors—in white, in color,
and in natural wood. Dark or light, they can
open or they can slide.

Whether a curtain fabric is plain or patterned depends entirely on the room scheme.
We do not go in for heavy linings and inter-
linings. If we are using silk or, indeed, acetate,
we normally do not line the curtains at all but
have inner curtains or shades to filter light.

Some people like full curtains, others
prefer them stricter, with less volume. This
decision also depends on the fabrics used,
whether silk taffeta, cotton, or linen, and, as
ever, on the window type. In historic or
traditional houses we might use swags and
valances, which should be distinctive, done
with a flourish and, sometimes, a smile. If
you are to have grand curtains, the grander
the better. In contemporary houses, fabric
shades or wooden slatted blinds are usually
de rigueur, but there are no fast rules. **❞**

Whether a curtain fabric
is plain or patterned
depends entirely on the
room scheme

John Stefanidis

KEITH IRVINE & JASON BELL

Keith Irvine, pictured here on the right, was born in Scotland and studied interior design at London's Royal College of Art. He served his apprenticeship under John Fowler, then started his own decorating business in the United States. His clients have included the Frick and Kennedy families, Cary Grant, and Diana Ross. Jason Bell (on the left) became interested in interior design at a young age as his mother was always "dabbling with decorating." He studied marketing and interior design at the University of Alabama, and is now a full partner of the newly named company Irvine, Fleming, Bell, LLC.

66 John Fowler was an omnivorous reader who absorbed so much of the detail and progression of curtain design. He bought many old eighteenth-century costumes and had them cut carefully apart. In this way, he could observe the cuts and stitching of gathered flounces, swags, and floating panels. This led to the rediscovery of pinked edges on ruffles and unusual braids and trims, such as the fan-edging Colefax & Fowler still sells.

KEITH IRVINE

Colefax & Fowler was a brilliant apprenticeship for me and stood me in very good stead when I came to America and started my own business. Though I am a traditionalist and classicist, American life has opened my eyes and enthusiasms to a much wider and more open approach to decoration. My first consideration has always been to make the room work brilliantly. Today, people want as much natural light to flood into their rooms as possible and much less fussy detail. I prefer plain fabrics used with stripes, accented with some pattern, and I tend to use pure cotton, voiles, and silk taffetas in abundance. The design must be suitable to the house. I've done curtains hung on Indian spears for a ranch house and *portières* in a Victorian house; and I'll use screens and shutters if I'm working in Florida or California. Suitability to the purpose is what curtains are all about.

JASON BELL

I take in the architecture first. I believe window treatments must not fight the architecture, or vice versa. I enjoy sitting in a space, looking at how the atmosphere changes at different times of the day. It's the use of the room and the atmosphere of the space that dictate my initial approach. My starting point is usually a general agreement on these factors with the clients, and then I begin questioning myself on how I can break the mold of what is expected.

I like using solid plain colors, stripes, and textured fabrics, and I like to add interjections of the great classics. By that, I mean fabrics such as chintz and toile de Jouy, and designs such as batik, because most of the clients I work with appreciate a splash of chintz here or there. I prefer mixing plain fabrics with patterns, although I think some spaces look best when there is no mixing at all and everything is the same.

I sense a desire for something different, for new ideas to be incorporated with the classics of design. Take valances, for instance, which are ripe for reinterpretation. I think they've been forgotten, which is a shame, because they can provide clever solutions to many difficult window treatments. Valances in the twenty-first century are about to get a new meaning—at least they will when I have finished with them! Throughout the history of art and design, a group of people pop up every twenty or thirty years and change things, and I believe the young designers of today are on the verge of creating another new look. **"**

> It's the use of the room and the atmosphere of the space that dictate the initial approach— and then we begin to break the mold of what's expected

ARTHUR DUNNAM OF JED JOHNSON ASSOCIATES

Arthur Dunnam is pictured on the right here, with, on the left, the late Jed Johnson, founder of the firm that Dunnam joined in 1986 and where he has been design director since 1997. His interior design projects are in diverse styles—from period restorations to contemporary penthouses—and include many individualistic houses in the Hamptons, ranging from British Arts and Crafts to Swedish neoclassical. His work exhibits meticulous attention to detail and respect for the architectural integrity of the buildings that contain his designs.

> 66 My general philosophy is exactly that of Jed Johnson, our founder— window treatments are an extension of the mood, tone, and style of the interior. If the residence is contemporary and restrained, the windows must convey the same clean simplicity, they must be appropriate to their setting.

STYLE AND INNOVATION

Jed Johnson revealed to me the seductive quality of sheer wool fabric. There is nothing that drapes more beautifully. Heavy silk taffeta looks incredibly rich and can be perfectly suited to both traditional and contemporary interiors. Embroidered and appliquéd fabrics are also a favorite. The more serious the room, the simpler the fabric. We generally prefer quiet but luxurious fabrics, and add visual interest with embroidery, appliqué, trimmings, or hardware.

If we are working on a period project, we pull out all the stops—valances, swags and tails, fringes, and tassels—if the formality of the rooms and the lifestyle of the client warrant it. In New York's Dakota building, for instance, which has lofty volumes of space in each room and highly decorative interior architecture, we have used *portière* curtains to add a softness and coziness. Although there must be a cohesive mood that flows throughout the residence, we use different types of drapes in different rooms. A subtle rhythm should envelop the principal rooms, created by varying certain elements and retaining others.

The most way-out window treatment we ever did was a few years ago on a project Jed had on Fifth Avenue with an enormous window in the master bathroom. The apartment was extremely restrained decoratively, and Jed struggled with the appropriate way to address this window, without it looking fussy or over-clinical. He came up with an ingenious idea to recreate a molded crystal floral screen by René Lalique. The final installation was stunning. It seems so appropriate that most people think it is original to the room.

WINDOW CHECKLISTS

My checklist includes the following practical elements. Determine the window treatments in tandem with the development of architectural drawings, so that moldings and details can be configured to accommodate the window treatment in a way that looks seamless. If a room is being paneled, allow room in the stiles that abut the window for the curtains to stack each side without obscuring portions of the paneling. Know exactly how your curtain hardware will mount. Existing architectural conditions can often be dealt with by using complex custom mounting brackets and

TOP

A sumptuous silk tassel tieback and braided edging adorn glorious jacquard dress curtains for a dining room, also illustrated on the right. When it comes to trimmings, the policy of Jed Johnson Associates is to do it right or not to do it at all.

ABOVE

Elegantly draped curtains, with elaborate tails that are swagged to form a self-valance, hang simply from a gilded rod—a brilliant solution for a tall, wide window.

RIGHT

A view of the dining room that has the tasseled tiebacks above shows the full majesty of the imposing curtains and their deep-pleated valances. The curtains take the eye up like soaring pillars to the elaboration at the top.

gold-painted version of the real thing, as it brings the whole room down. The same goes for trimmings. Do it right or don't do it at all. If you have a beautiful view, don't obscure it with a fussy window treatment.

Finally, if you're a designer, listen to your client; if you're a client, listen to your designer. You both have valuable points and opinions and the relationship should always be about collaboration. Politeness coupled with intense persistence was a path that Jed Johnson never strayed from in his relationships with clients, and it is only one of his many qualities as a designer that we feel still define us as a firm. **"**

> The more serious the room, the simpler the fabric. We generally prefer quiet but luxurious fabrics and add interest with embroidery or trimmings

Arthur Dunnum

ABOVE

A lovely mixture of plain and embroidered silk is created for this imposing bedroom, dominated by a magnificent four-poster. The fabric hangs straight from neat, inverted, pleat valances. The precise tailoring and the absence of frills give the room a masculine edge.

RIGHT

A single, tied back curtain separates a hallway from a corridor, giving the space a hint of mystery and surprise. The heavy striped cotton fabric with matching fringe adds an exotic touch to the Art Nouveau interior style.

supports. If your windows are tall, the curtains will be heavy, so make sure the mounting brackets have adequate blocking behind the wall surface. This is best done before the hand painted wallpaper has been installed! If you can, move air vents so curtains don't stack on them. Blinds and sheers should rest between the window glass and the air vents, allowing air into the room when the blinds are drawn.

A design checklist concentrates on the following considerations. Address the unalterable givens in the room and select your curtain design accordingly. If windows align awkwardly—butting into corners, for instance—do not exacerbate the situation with masses of fabric stacking into a corner. Rods and rings, decorative valance boards, and the like, must be an extension of the architectural tone and quality of the room. If you have the good fortune to have a wonderfully detailed and refined room and you can't afford beautiful accessories, then go the simple route. Do not try and pass off a molded resin,

Colleen Bery's curtains have a totally traditional look, but the antique appeal of the fabric, which looks like an old tapestry, is an illusion—it's hand painted silk. She uses pale, restrained, and faded colors that blend into the walls, with coordinated shades.

Keller Donavan likes his curtains to look "tailored, neat, and jaunty," as does this stunning, restrained use of clean, striped fabric, which is cleverly pleated and draped over the high poles.

Colleen Bery in London, who makes hand painted curtains that look as if they have grown old gracefully along with the room. "My designs are perhaps less fussy now than they were," she told me. "I don't use trim on curtains, but I do make valances."

REINVENTING THE CLASSIC

So how do you reinvent a classic? Today, many designers use less fussy fabrics, revel in pure color and texture, and add sharper, tailored touches. "My aim is make curtains that look timeless," says Colleen Bery—and for me, that says it all, because real classics never go out of style. Talking to these designers has taught me that it takes a lot of expertise to confidently ignore the vagaries of fashion and create a look that will last.

CLASSIC TALES

The lessons learned from these master classes in the classic are about how to drag those grand, draped curtains with their swags and tiebacks firmly into the twenty-first century. The ways of doing so, however, are not straightforward. For example, I asked all the designers I interviewed if they felt that elaborate treatments had had their day. The general consensus was a resounding "maybe," depending on the circumstances.

A SIMPLER STYLE

I spoke with the influential Keller Donavan in New York, who describes his style as Fresh American Classic. "Certain rooms," he told me, "need good, elaborate valances—period homes, for instance. But I think we should try and reinvent them." I also spoke with

There is **absolutely nothing simple** about achieving this wonderful look, because the simpler you want things to be, the more difficult they become. Everything is visible, every detail commands attention, and therefore everything has to be beyond perfect. It is not a look that is as simple to achieve as it is calming to contemplate, and consequently it is not something easily embarked upon by an amateur. To be successful at minimalism requires an in-depth knowledge of architecture and a true understanding of detail and quality. Simplicity has always been about the **elegance of a line** and elegance has to be sweated over.

Each of the designers in this section brings something of their own to this most rigorous of design disciplines. Some use blocks of related color, while others make a feature of the interplay of **contrasting textures** such as silk and leather. One element that pulls these designs together is a common thread of a sense of unity that they display. There is little in the way of tension evident in the designs, but there is still an energy that is expressed in the lack of fuss, the sharp detailing of seams, and the considered placement of objects. With little else to distract the eye, attention focuses on **form and shape**, and window treatments are a significant part of the style. The simple look is about letting in the light and letting the windows of the house speak for themselves.

Simple, uncluttered style is a twenty-first-century ideal. Today, everyone wants less baggage in life. Having lived through the design excesses of the late twentieth century and found the results wanting, both in style and in substance, people yearn to live more simply. It is time to chuck out the clutter and the frills and to remember the past, not through an attic full of meaningless junk, but by spotlighting one **exquisite and thoughtful** piece. "Simple" is a style about eliminating rather than adding—but in the hands of the designers featured here, it is certainly not about paring down at the expense of comfort or beauty.

Simple

KELLY HOPPEN

Sheer style that incorporates calm and balance describes the work of this innovative interior designer. Taking her inspiration from both western and eastern traditions, Kelly Hoppen creates interior schemes that blend with the natural world. Her international commissions include the design of first-class cabins for British Airways, corporate office spaces, and private homes. She has designed her own collection of interior accessories, including rugs, wall-to-wall carpets, paints, fabrics, bed linen, and window accessories. She is the author of four interior design books that describe her style and vision.

❝ The way I think about curtains has changed. Years ago it was about using masses of fabric to cover windows, whereas today it's about light. People are more aware of light now; they want curtains that are sheer and translucent, not lined and interlined. There's a trend toward simplifying your life, away from the full swish and all the accompanying frills and tassels.

ORIGINAL IDEAS

One of my responses to this demand has been to adapt the idea of the Japanese *shoji* screen and use it as a window treatment. Traditionally, *shoji* panels were made of rice paper on bamboo frames and used as room dividers. I install the framework in front of the window and then tailor inter-changeable fabric panels that attach with Velcro. It's a brilliant way to deal with windows, because you can effect change so easily. One day you might want some gray linen, or felt, or leather mixed with linen, another day all-white or all-sheer. I have clients who have five different sets of panels. I continue to innovate with this idea, and I'm making room dividers to match the window shades. I've used fabric trapped between two sheets of glass, and at

the moment we're sandblasting perspex and adding lacquer stripes. I love the flatness and the linear look of panels.

You've got to keep exploring new avenues. It would be interesting to see a modern take on a pair of over-the-top, old-fashioned curtains. I'd create the effect entirely with the volume of a translucent fabric, with no borders or tassels. I'm working on a set of curtains with metallic voile on the inside, chocolate brown denim linen on top and a massive valance of leather fringing. It's not my usual style, but it's amazing.

BEDROOM WINDOWS

You need darkness when you sleep, so for bedrooms I've started making the shade the thicker entity on the window; most people do

ABOVE
The bay window of a dining room is dressed in Kelly's favorite fabric, a fine parachute silk that hangs perfectly and retains its shape. It is simply caught with clip-on rings on a slim metal rod, leaving the lovely arches of the period windows clearly visible.

RIGHT
The sides of this bay window have been paneled for use as closets, leaving the central window to let in light and air. A simple Roman blind of natural linen with a darker insert stripe is clean, crisp, and minimally decorative.

TEXTURES

I start designing with fabric and textures. I gather together a selection of fabrics, and at the beginning I won't decide which goes where. The fabric you use on the windows will always be the largest expanse you see. It will completely dominate the room, so you've got to get it right. Then I take a large piece of that fabric and look at it vertically, because it's amazing how it changes according to the plane it's seen in. Shot fabrics like taffetas can give you a big surprise.

I'm definitely not a pattern person, but I will border fabrics and make bands across them. For instance, I would use a wonderful expensive silk bordered with gray flannel or wool. I do very big borders at the bottom and the side, or a band across the middle to break it up. If you border a very fine fabric with a thicker one like velvet, you have to worry technically about how it will sit. I got the inspiration for visible stitching by watching a sail-maker at work. With stitching like that, you can control how the different fabrics relate.

I love linens, scrims, and sheers, and if you always weight them, they will sit beautifully, but my favorite fabrics of all time are fine parachute fabrics with viscose in them that really hold their shape. We've just done a wonderful curved bay for an apartment in Paris, using the thinnest and finest parachute

ABOVE LEFT

Beautiful but simple, the sheer outer curtains here tumble like a waterfall from an elegant metal pole. They let in light while raising the eye to the ceiling and providing a strong vertical element to the room. The Roman blind behind the sheer is of natural linen, trimmed with leather.

ABOVE RIGHT

A shimmering fall of self-striped white sheer fabric filters light into this calm bedroom. Behind the curtains, a linen Roman blind stands ready to provide darkness and privacy.

it the other way round, with heavy curtains and a sheer shade. I don't use blackout shades, but a fabric so thick it has the same effect. I use fabrics such as leather and fake suede, because I like to shock with an unexpected mix of materials. In front of the blind, I often include a sheer in a fabric so soft you have to put tiny weights in it, so you can manipulate it, lift it like the hem of a ball-gown, move a weight here and there and sculpt it like glass.

Shutters look very good in children's rooms. You can make them as a solid block of fabric, such as suede or felt, and fit them exactly into the window. Then it's either dark or light, and there are no fussy bits or blind mechanisms to worry about. I like each area of the house to have the same personality, so if I'm dealing with a whole floor of bedrooms, I like them to relate to each other in some way, because I think spaces should read through open doors.

RIGHT
A dining room window is dressed with *shoji* panels, hung from a top track, which move sideways. The covering of these panel—here, a beige linen—is attached with velcro, so the fabric can easily be removed and another substituted to suit the prevailing mood.

BELOW
In Kelly's own bedroom, in a traditional period house with decorative plaster cornices, white linen curtains hang in the bay window. The valance, that hides the tracks, is a simple wooden box, upholstered in white satin. Elegant shades of thick taupe linen underneath ensure privacy.

fabric. I wanted one curtain hanging on each side, meeting in the center, but because you have to have more than two sets of brackets on the pole, the movement becomes cumbersome. I'm waiting for someone to invent a curved pole with no visible means of support.

I use a lot of synthetic leather and suede. I rarely use the real thing, because it comes

in hides, and unless you want to make a feature of the joins, you get a better effect with synthetics. I tend to make a feature of joins in any case, perhaps using widths of flat linen joined with voile pleats. I've also been using very thick fabrics, such as heavy wool, punching holes in them so the light shines through in filigree patterns.

It's sharp detailing and the interplay of textures, such as those of silk and leather, that make plain-colored curtains look interesting. One color with different textures is just as empowering as different colors. In the end, making curtains is rather like making couture clothes. There's a correct weight and texture for every purpose and every effect you want to achieve. If I can, I'll put curtains on a rod. I love the sound of curtains drawing, which is why I love iron rods and iron rings. I always think they sound like the entry curtain of a restaurant in France. Rods and poles have character, too. If you compare making curtains to making clothes, the curtain pole takes on the role of the shoe. "

I'm definitely not a pattern person, but I will border fabrics and make bands across them. I use a wonderful expensive silk bordered with gray flannel or with wool

> 66 The first thing I want is clean windows that let the light in as clearly as possible. For a long time, windows were seen as part of the exterior of the house, but they are now definitely part of the interior, integrated into the space. I like to consider what comes through that window, like the shadows that fall into the room; and if there's a grid of glazing bars, how that repeats on the floor.

VICENTE WOLF

A major player in the world of contemporary design for over twenty years, Vicente Wolf heads his own company, through which he explores his guiding principles of integrity and simplicity. The company's commissions are diverse, ranging from stores in Hong Kong and Chicago, to private residences in New York and Beverly Hills. Vicente Wolf also travels as a teacher and lecturer and has recently opened a showroom of antiques and accessories collected on his travels. His work appears frequently in the pages of international design and interiors magazines.

ARCHITECTURE

The treatment of a window really depends on how you want the space to read. If the amount of light and shadow gives the room a very open feel, which is what I like, then I don't think a window treatment is required at all. For me, curtains are a purely architectural decision to deal with faults of the space in a decorative way. In an average house with not much going for it, a bare window points up the defects. You don't really want to see the lack of architecture. By softening the top of the window with fabric, you make it disappear into the wall, so it's no longer the focal point of the room.

Windows are part of the background. The ceiling, walls, window, and floor are the shell. A successful window is part of the four walls, even if it has the added feature of light or a view, and it still has to blend in. If the walls are white, then blinds of the same color white give a continuity of background. I'm always looking for a sense of the total environment.

I like big windows, the larger the better, which means if they don't come up to the ceiling then I try to elongate them. I always take the window shades up to the ceiling so there's no empty space above them. You could say you can never have enough height, but there's a limit. If the windows are too big, it throws your proportion out of scale, so you tweak to make it intimate and use curtains to play out the verticality of the space.

ABOVE
Here is a very strong case for no curtains at all, because the windows are beautifully symmetrical sashes and the room needs all the light it can get. Painted black, they are frames for the city view.

LEFT
The curtain here has become part of the architecture. It's a soft column of plain cream fabric that complements the strong shapes of the beams and the horizontal lines of the shelving.

RIGHT
The bedroom area of this loft space has a simple white shade at the window. In order to inject interest into the architecture, Vicente has put the bed on a diagonal in front of a false wall.

LIGHT

Sixty percent of my work is in Manhattan and I've learned to respect what you see out of the window. We have enormous, magnificent views and you don't want to obscure them. If clients want privacy, I use transparent fabrics that let the light through but obscure the view from the outside. Of course, there are situations where you get too much light. I did a job in Taos, New Mexico recently where the light that came in was blinding, heating the whole place up, so I used very fine wool that really solved the problem.

There are some rooms where you want a feeling of warmth and luxury, such as dining-rooms. I've always thought of dining rooms as useless when you're not eating, all hard edges and empty chairs waiting for something to happen, so I use curtains as a way of softening the sounds and giving the room some kind of depth. But I wouldn't single out the window; I'd use fabric all the way round the room, so it becomes part of the background, part of the architecture of the space.

FABRIC

People associate extravagant yardage, particularly for curtains, with luxury and refinement. I think it's an old trick that people are comfortable with, but if they come to me to style their homes, then they're already not expecting that I will provide such designs. If we do curtains, they are very straight and vertical. If they are used to be decorative, we make them from wool, silk, or taffeta; and if they are to filter light, we use light and transparent fabric. I love polished wool, which has a sheen and a lot of body. I love taffeta, particularly the swishing noise it makes, and I use sheers, a lot of sheers. I tend not to use color at windows, although in a very dark apartment, I might use creamy linen to soften light in bright spaces when the light shines through. Alternatively, I might decide to use a soft, sky-blue fabric, which gives a sense of the sky outside.

I don't like open-weave fabrics or patterns. For me design is about form, shape, and blocks of color playing against each other. I think the moment you start using patterns on pieces of furniture or windows, you're always seeing the pattern itself rather than the shape of the piece. But if the chair or the curtain or the blind is one solid color, then it changes as the light hits it; and if you see it against another color, it changes again. I like rooms that are not set; I like evolution and fluidity.

RIGHT
The pleated cream curtains at these immense windows park against the flanking walls, substituting for paintings or other decorations. Privacy is cleverly achieved by using roller blinds that pull up from the bottom, ensuring seclusion where needed but allowing light to enter from the top.

PAST AND PRESENT

The American interior has been accused of being static. I think this comes from the insecurity of always wanting to have history along, to have a past. But wherever American design has broken ground, as it did in the 1950s, then it becomes very innovative. Perhaps because Europe has more diversity, people there have the confidence to keep evolving, adding to the bits-and-pieces their parents and grandparents had. If I'm working with a traditional space, I like to respect the past but deal with it in the present. I deal with a historic interior in a much more minimal way than a contemporary space—I paint it white. It's the contemporary spaces that need more attention to detail. I find that putting a room together is like doing a jigsaw puzzle. You want to find things that fit together, so when it's finished you see the total picture, but when you take it apart, you're looking at beautiful pieces in their own right.

STYLE

I'd say my style was a blending of elements, old and new—1940s, eighteenth-century French, rustic, and smooth—that give my work an unpretentious quality, even in rich spaces. My work is about comfort, not attitude, and my rooms don't overwhelm because I don't think people should be in competition with their living spaces. If you have a chair you can't sit on, it just becomes "look but don't touch." I remember as a child in Cuba never being allowed to go into the living room, which was just to look at, and it was so annoying. I mean, why not use it? I think spaces should house people. 99

a successful window is part of the four walls. Even if it has the added feature of light or a view, it still has to blend in. I'm always looking for a sense of the total environment

" I used to be seized by the same insecurity about window design as everyone else. I'm an architect by training and I was completely flummoxed by curtain jargon. Goblet headings, pinch pleats, French headings—none of it meant anything to me. I was at the mercy of curtain makers and I found the control of the design passing out of my hands. So I educated myself. Now the mystique has been stripped away and I know what curtains are for—to control light and, to a certain extent, privacy.

DESIGN PRINCIPLES

I make decisions about curtains very early on, partly because they take a long time to make, but mainly because the wall treatment is very dependent on the curtains and vice versa—they've got to work together. I know that I feel more comfortable in a room that has curtains. We are all aware that we don't want people looking in, we want to walk around unobserved. If you walk into a house in which the walls are upholstered, there's a wonderful feeling of comfort, and curtains also help the acoustics and the overall ambience of a room. It is also important that

DAVID COLLINS

David Collins was born and grew up on the coast outside Dublin, Ireland. After studying architecture and traveling Europe widely, he established his architecture and design company in 1985, delivering a one-stop design service to ensure that an initial concept is both developed and carried through to its final stages. This work is characterized by a fine attention to detail, texture, and technique and to the progressive use of color and light in interior schemes. David Collins' portfolio contains a glittering array of private residences and some of the finest restaurants in the UK, a number of which have won him design awards.

THIS PAGE

A detail of the curtains in the garden room of a London house designed by David Collins, that are pictured opposite on the right. The curtains are of specially woven, white silk taffeta, tied back with magnificent silk tassels, one trimmed with feathers and the others given feathery fronds.

OPPOSITE RIGHT

The all-white garden room has an elegant Regency feel to it. These magnificent, column-like curtains are hung from a bronze pole. The expanse of taffeta has contrasting borders of celadon silk, and they hang like a dream.

OPPOSITE LEFT

A simple swoop of claret and black silk hangs from a metal rod. A trim of slate-colored silk velvet on the leading edge emphasizes the elegant curve that this curtain brings to a hallway otherwise dominated by straight lines.

LEFT AND BELOW.
In this large, elegant room with fireplaces at both ends, Collins has designed wonderfully simple curtains in a gold-and-ecru circular geometric fabric. It complements the gilded plasterwork that is such a feature of the room. The curtains hang, column-like, from French-pleated headings. The under curtains are simple, open-weave linen sheers, in keeping with the contemporary furnishings.

curtains harmonize with the room. All too frequently, you see beautiful interiors—wonderful furniture, exquisite art on the walls—but the curtains look as if they belong to another era. We all want to live more simply now, and that's reflected in the way curtain design has evolved. We don't want to swathe ourselves in swags, but we might want to dress ourselves up with the equivalent of designer accessories, which is why there's been an upsurge of interest in exotic *passementerie*.

People don't want big statements any more, they want curtains that function—you can't get away with elaborate installations held together with a staple-gun. I favor curtains that just touch the floor. I am not that keen on valances and I like simple rings. I think all the curtains in a house should be similar, but not identical, and because they should be related to the decoration, they should stay where they are when you move—you can never successfully re-hang curtains from one house to another.

CURTAINS AS ILLUSION

It's easy enough to make curtains for a perfectly proportioned window with access for tracks or rods. The real problems come from really awkward windows that are asymmetrical or wedged in a corner, or

arched or framed in a deep box. But here you can learn from stage-craft and set design, because with curtains you can create a bit of an illusion. They can compensate for architectural mistakes and give the impression of grandeur or simplicity, but you've got to have the confidence to do that. It's not just existing buildings that give designers headaches. Architects make glass buildings and leave the client and the designer to work out how to control light, heat, and privacy without it looking as if they've been hanging out the washing.

PLAIN TEXTURES

I work with plain fabrics mostly, because I get tired of patterns very quickly. There's always an exception, though, and I've recently used a Fortuny fabric with a mud-colored African batik design. I use silks and linens and a sprinkling of contemporary modern fabrics. I often use sheer under curtains, which I suppose are the modern equivalent of net curtains, and when I can't get what I want for a particular job, I get them woven myself, either here or in Asia.

I love texture. The raw linen used for scrims, for instance, inspired a fabric I had made that's softer than scrim but as chunky, and I like cheap raw silk because it absorbs color like no other fabric. The details are within the fabric for me, and they are quite subtle. I've used fabrics with tiny beads, canvas that's been painted and cracked, quilted silks, filmy silk edged with stiff organza, and even curtains made entirely from glass beads. No matter how expensive the fabric, I will probably spend more money on having the curtains made up and on hanging them properly. "

We all want to live more simply now, and that's reflected in the way curtain design has evolved

ABOVE
In a main bedroom, oyster silk and cotton satin curtains are recessed behind period carved and molded window reveals. The curtains are gathered high up in the Italian string style—the ripcord used for theatre curtains—giving them a jaunty, Regency look.

RIGHT
A strong case is made here for blinds as works of art. Tucked under the curved architrave, these unusual pull-up blinds are made from specially woven panels of sheer fabric with an intricate thread pattern. They are all the decoration the room needs.

EMILY TODHUNTER

This distinctive designer made her name in the 1980s with the witty and glamorous interiors of a nightclub in Manhattan and some of Britain's top restaurants. Her light-hearted approach to design, attention to detail, and use of delicious, understated colors have since attracted many international clients. In 1998, she was joined by Kate Earle, pictured with her here, and together they formed Todhunter Earle Ltd. in Chelsea, London. Their calm and sophisticated designs, inspired by Parisian interiors of the 1920s and 1930s, translate to commissions from contemporary urban lofts to rustic barn conversions.

" I don't have a design philosophy. I try not to think too hard or too deeply, but go with the flow, and I try not to impose my own style on my clients. I'd rather let the whole thing evolve and let the room happen to me, rather than let me happen to it.

We do a huge range of projects, from yachts to country house hotels, from Swiss chalets to London townhouses. I suppose the identifiable style is relaxed, simple, and not too decorated. It's lodged somewhere between modern and traditional, but not in limbo. I make references to tradition, particularly to comfort and a relaxed atmosphere, but my work has a cleaner, more contemporary look. I like to think it is the best of both worlds—clean, young, and energetic, but still educated, without being too clever.

ATMOSPHERICS

In approaching the window design, first I think about the furniture arrangements, because I want to get the atmosphere right and it's important to know how people move around the room and interact with each other. My next considerations are the view and ways in which to maximize the light, creating a space that will make people happy. If I'm doing a London house that looks out on a

TOP

Simple falls of pale fabric adorn the windows of a typical London townhouse. The signature of the simple look is to blend the windows into the walls in this way.

LEFT

In a drawing room, Emily has designed curtains of raw silk, fully lined with a synthetic silk fabric, which also trims the curtain with a wide band and prevents rapid deterioration from sunlight.

LEFT BELOW

This compact en suite bathroom has a simple sheer roller blind in a specially commissioned fabric. The subtle pattern ensures privacy, while letting in a pretty pattern of light.

RIGHT

There's a place for sentiment in the simple look. Here, a pair of antique gilded wooden valances – bought for Emily's first home, but which go with her everywhere – are given elegant raw silk and linen curtains.

garden square, there will be a view of black iron railings, sidewalks, and grass. I'll try and do something neutral in creams and beiges, colors that relate to the outside and draw your eye to the view without stopping short at the window. And then I'll make the curtains as elegant and simple as possible, so you don't really notice them, with maybe a translucent shade in silk or muslin to filter the light.

I don't like curtains to be too dominant. I like a simple, subdued look that doesn't detract from the view. I hate that standard, old-fashioned way of decorating, which was to ignore what the room was saying to you, to choose a chintz and then decorate a room around it. I very rarely use patterned fabrics for curtains, I'm more likely to use a patterned lining. In fact, I nearly always specify a patterned lining, so it's a nice surprise when you move the curtain aside or catch a tiny glimpse of something interesting.

My home looks out over a London square, so for the rooms on the street side of the house I've used a neutral palette of putty gray, beige, and cream. On the other side, which is north-facing, I have a dark room with just one window and a dull view, which makes it tricky. In order to move the

ABOVE

A detail of the two track system used for the curtains illustrated on the right demonstrates the joy of having two independent layers that pull across easily—you can mix and match pattern and plain.

RIGHT

The lower-ground floor of this London home opens out to a sunny courtyard. There are two sets of curtains at the massive window, both unlined and each with its own track and pulley system. The top fabric is a silky, flimsy orange and cream geometric and the under curtains are of matching plain orange silk.

eye away from the window, I've used a true red on the walls to warm the room up and I've tried to lose the curtains by using fabric of the same color. That way, the window doesn't jump out at you and create another block of color; and when the curtains are drawn, the window simply isn't there.

When we design our collections, we do wallpapers and fabrics that match so we can make curtains that you don't really notice. On one of my projects I again had a room with one window—a very ugly window with a very ugly view. So I gave the room a Japanese theme. I blocked off the window with blackout shades and used a Japanese screen in front. It was like building a fake window in front of the window, making a virtue out of a vice.

FUTURE REALITIES

I think curtain design is getting much simpler. The complicated swags and tails and trims have all gone, and I don't regret their passing. I might just possibly be persuaded to produce swags for a pair of huge, tall windows in a stately home, but, on the other hand, maybe not even then. People's lives are so much more stressful now, so they want to get

home and find comfort, calm, and relaxation. People want their houses to work, to be functional, and because rooms are multi-purpose, you have to strive for balance. You can't have elaborate confections, spindly gilt furniture, and distracting fabrics in a room that trebles as kitchen, dining room, and family room. It's time to get real. 99

the style is relaxed, simple, and not too decorated. It's lodged somewhere between modern and traditional, but not in limbo

Emily Todhunter.

ABOVE

A calm, Japanese-style bedroom is achieved with strong horizontal lines, a total absence of clutter and *shoji* screens at the window. The only pattern is on the walls, but the windows, sectioned into horizontal panels, retain their interest.

ABOVE LEFT

In this small powder room, a combination of three fabrics make separate shades. The rich color of the principal shade is for drama, the next is a rough, decorative sheer for texture and light, while the inner blind is absolutely plain, designed for privacy.

MIMMI O'CONNELL

A Swiss citizen born in Italy, Mimmi O'Connell has been based in London since 1970 and is an international design consultant. Her current projects include two houses in London's Belgravia, a palace in the medina of Marrakesh, and a house in the Bahamas. Her work has involved private residences in all parts of the world, including such far-flung locations as Lithuania, Indonesia, Kuwait, and Argentina, and the spaces she has designed range from city apartments to beach houses and farmhouses. She is a director of a number of design companies in London and Switzerland.

ABOVE
The plain white walls form a suitable background for the restrained, uncluttered, ethnic look of this room, in which all attention is focused on the fantastic curtains. There is no elaboration at the top, the curtains simply hang on rings from plain metal rods.

LEFT
Mimmi is the absolute queen of the layered look. She never gets it wrong. Here she has draped over curtains of blue-and-cream silk over burgundy under curtains that just spill onto the ground in huge, exuberant puddles.

BELOW RIGHT
This curtain gives the illusion of having a valance but, in fact, it has none at all, just a flap of the curtain material doubled over at the top and edged with binding tape. Light is filtered through antique Japanese bamboo blinds.

66 When I design curtains, my first look is at the proportions of the windows and at the light coming through. I don't have a rigid set of rules to apply in every situation; I adapt to what is required. In fact, I quite like rooms in which the curtains aren't the most important part of the decoration. If you're a collector, the curtains have to be a backdrop.

DESIGN VARIETY

My curtains are generally unlined and simple. I layer fabrics instead of lining them and normally edge them with bias borders or with binding tapes. The fabrics can be important. I like rich, extravagant, voluptuous silks flirting with light and shadows; velvets, wools, antique textiles, superb embroidery; Indian or French linen, and toile de Jouy. I'm mostly associated with curtains made of layers and layers of fabulous silks, but beautiful as they are, such curtains take a certain discipline to live with. For one thing, they can't be drawn; and people often don't realize just how expensive it is to achieve such an effect.

I'm not using serious valances any more, even in authentic period houses. Fun valance treatments need not be fixed, but can be part of the curtain, sometimes in a different fabric, with lovely binding. There are things that I wouldn't ever do again (such as balloon blinds). Quite a nice idea is emerging, a way of making curtains using a limited amount of plain fabric that is pinned up asymmetrically, which is very French Empire. Strictly speaking, it is not new, but is an ageless idea that looks very modern.

I'm not in favor of pomposity. People approach me because they see what I've done and they know to expect a degree of surprise. My curtains are not for low budgets —actually, some are atrociously expensive!

UNDERSTATEMENTS

Because my curtains are not made to close, I use under curtains or a blackout shade. I'm using a lot of *sudari*, which are traditional Japanese shades made out of very thin bamboo, filtering light beautifully. The bindings are made out of silk, and the fittings have wonderful metal hooks. I don't mind them coming in small sizes, because I can use two side by side. They are chic and look fantastic under silk curtains. Medieval rush matting looks great at a window, too. You can make huge blinds with it, like having a rug on the wall. It's what they use in Mediterranean countries as awnings to keep out the glare of the sun.

If the view is stunning and you're not overlooked—and the room is not a bedroom—then I quite like the idea of having no window treatment at all. But it doesn't work unless you have a fabulous view, like an artwork in a frame. It requires courage, because your window is going to be naked. 99

I'm not in favor of pomposity. People approach me because they see what I've done and they know to expect a degree of surprise

TOP

The layered look is taken to the edge. The outer curtain of white linen is tied to a pole and has a thick striped border on the leading edge. The under curtain of blue check hangs on rings on a separate, thinner, rod behind the main pole.

ABOVE

The fresh mix of plains, striped ticking, and checks continues in the rest of the room. Mimmi has turned this small vaulted space into an inviting little bedroom.

ABOVE

A wonderfully elaborate bed and a pair of gilded chairs would be swamped with a traditional curtain treatment. Mimmi has used three fabrics for these simple, tie-headed curtains—thin and thick striped ticking sewn together in strips with a plain white linen underneath.

ABOVE

Hand embroidered crewelwork such as this can cost a fortune, but luckily, plenty of good-looking, machine-embroidered fabrics are available that can achieve a similar look.

RIGHT

A wonderful baldaquin bed is left unadorned by curtains. At the window, sheer linen under-curtains play with the light beneath a generous drop of white crewelwork, unlined so that the embroidered pattern is seen as a shadow.

Simple bamboo blinds have their fixings hidden well above the window so they can be pulled clear, leaving the owners of this clean, architectural bedroom with an unobstructed view of Brooklyn Bridge. Bamboo has a warmth to it that is ideal for use in bedrooms.

A window in a simple country bathroom is not overlooked, but when privacy is required, there's a totally opaque white Roman blind, which can be pulled right up onto the space above the window.

Perihan Al-Uzri designed this striking bedroom in a London apartment. She used bamboo blinds created by Sabina Fay Braxton of Paris. The blinds are edged in silk and have pulls of real coral. Underneath hangs a bright red silk blind, a perfect foil for the bamboo.

SIMPLE CONCLUSIONS

The designers who have provided us with master classes in the simple all agreed that the function of a window is to let in light and air. It is not there to provide an excuse for an in-your-face fashion statement.

Curtains should be discreet backdrops. Vicente Wolf didn't want his rooms to have "an overwhelming personality, because I don't think people should be in competition with their living space." David Collins told us that on the road from architecture to interior decoration he had learned that the purpose of curtains was to control light and privacy. "It's important that curtains harmonize with the room," he said. "All too often, you see beautiful interiors, but the curtains look as if they belong to another era."

WORKING WITH THE ENVIRONMENT
Mimmi O'Connell's first concern is with "the proportions of windows and the light that comes through them." If necessary, Mimmi will use her curtains to correct the proportions of the window, as will Vicente Wolf. In fact, if a window works well in the space, Vicente will often leave it alone to speak for itself. "For me," he says, "using curtains is purely an architectural decision to deal with faults of the space in a decorative way."

Emily Todhunter has strong feelings about views out through the windows and aims to create treatments in neutral colors—ones that relate to the outside—in order to draw the eye to the view. "I make curtains as elegant and simple as possible, so you don't really notice them," she told me. Mimmi is happy to leave a stunning aspect completely unadorned, but she sounds a note of caution that bare windows don't work "unless you have a fabulous view like an artwork in a frame."

THE COMPLEXITY OF FABRICS
For these designers, the texture of a fabric is far more important than its color or pattern. Kelly Hoppen starts her design decisions with the fabric, gathering together samples without making any decision about what goes where. "I'm definitely not a pattern person," she reminded me. "But I will border fabrics and make bands across them." Perihan Al-Uzri also works with a modern, simple approach to fabric, relying on borders and bands rather than patterns. "I like plain fabrics, and I like rough natural textures, like linen," she says. "I like contrast—a

For this sweeping bay window in a period London house, Perihan Al-Uzri has chosen an elegant understatement, allowing the architecture to shine. She uses fine gauze Roman blinds, stiffened with wooden sticks and bound with leather.

leather valance and leather tiebacks on sheer curtains, or bamboo blinds bordered in silk." Emily Todhunter is not committed to pattern either. "I very rarely use patterned fabrics for curtains," she admits. "I'm more likely to use a patterned lining… when you move the curtain aside you catch a tiny glimpse of something interesting." David Collins, too, owned up to preferring plain fabrics because "I get tired of patterns very quickly."

Favored fabrics are linens, cottons, silks, and fine sheers. Perihan Al-Uzri enthused that "the sheers you can get now are amazing. Just about anything you can dream up, you can do technically and I think that's why interior design is so exciting and moving in a different direction now."

The surprise element of the simple style comes from the interplay of textures that it incorporates with its fabrics. Kelly, for instance, uses shot taffeta, synthetic suede and leather; and she makes shades and screens with everything from etched glass to rice paper. Mimmi uses blinds of bamboo and of rush matting. Vicente has discovered polished wool and also uses a lot of taffeta, both for its looks and the wonderful swishing sound it makes; and David Collins uses fabrics sewn with beads, painted canvas that has been crackle-glazed, and quilted silks.

SIMPLE SOPHISTICATION

I think I had assumed, before I talked to these designers at length, that the understated, white roller blind was the key window treatment for the minimalist interior. Now I have learned that minimalism has moved on and evolved into a style that is altogether softer and full of subtle surprises. As the style comes of age in the twenty-first century, it exhibits a sophistication that seems light years away from its early beginnings.

TOP LEFT

Nico Rensch designed this simple New York space featuring slim Venetian blinds with wide tapes, that look very vertical and architectural. There's a love of light evident in the way the shadows of the glazing bars fall into the room.

ABOVE LEFT

A cool white bedroom has a touch of the tropical, emphasized by the chunky bamboo four-poster bed. The roller window blinds are made of three panels of creamy sheer linen. The center panel can be rolled up to clear the opening section of the window.

TOP RIGHT

In a stunning, double-height, book-lined sitting room on Long Island, Nico Rensch has used white muslin Roman blinds—essential here, because there is nowhere for bulky fabric to park within the reveals.

ABOVE RIGHT

This is a stunningly simple idea. A white roller blind rolls up from the baseboard rather than down from the top, ensuring privacy while light streams in from above. It's the same principal as the café curtain, but not nearly so fussy.

The designers who direct the master classes here have a sense of drama. They are generally from the same decorative arts background as those who make classic drapes, but they have used their skills differently, achieving quite startling results. They play with their knowledge and consistently bend and **break the rules**—but you can't do that unless you know exactly what the rules are.

These creators have an innate **sense of the dramatic**. From the shell of a room, they can compose an entire family history, much as an art director might dress a set for a long-running family saga. Starting from an eighteenth-century, classical base, they will imagine which much-loved pieces of furniture would have grown shabby and scuffed with age, which items would have been thrown out or recovered or remodeled, and what little touches might have been added over the years. This is where you find Fortuny silks mixed with chain mail, sheer silk curtains trimmed with crystal drops, hand painted murals, recreations of Chinese silk wallpapers, and other heady examples of theatrical **flamboyance**.

Dramatic style is flattering, both to the ego and the skin tones. In your own personal theater you can shine. It is in interiors such as these that I have seen mirrored tops on dining tables, the better to reflect the shimmer of silver, glass, and jewelry, and lighting effects borrowed from film sets, in which everyone looks glamorous. The stage is bordered by **dramatic sweeps** of curtain, framing the action taking place in the room.

These are the designers to turn to if your home is cursed with less-than-perfect window proportions, because there is nothing like a sense of mischief and a thorough grounding in classicism to equip you to become a master or mistress of illusion. A window treatment in the hands of a designer with a sense of drama can be made to command attention by taking center stage, or adopt the role of a supporting character. Whichever part they play, the curtains featured here are always **unpredictable and surprising**.

Dramatic

ANTONY LITTLE

Co-founder of Osborne & Little, one of Britain's leading design companies, Antony Little heads a team of designers producing about twelve new wallpaper and fabric designs each year. Inspiration comes from a broad range of sources—Indian and Oriental art, gardens, heraldry and the natural world, for example. Antony's fabric designs fuse the classical with the contemporary, adding fresh twists with unusual colors and sophisticated weaves. Osborne & Little have showrooms in London, New York, Chicago, Washington, Paris, and Munich.

66 The first consideration is what a curtain is for. There are two strands—the purely decorative and, more importantly, the functional. Do you need to cut out light and do you need privacy? If you don't, and you have great architecture, then you don't need curtains. Functional needs are harder to define now because people no longer live in a formal way, but have all-purpose rooms that are harder to pin down.

ABOVE

This small bedroom in the roof of Antony's tiny country cottage is a riot of color and pattern. A swathe of fabric suspended across an entire wall is caught back to reveal a staircase beyond, dominated by a large tree that is crucial to the structure.

GETTING STARTED

Although I'm not a decorator, I am often asked how I start to decorate and get the ideas going. My answer is to try and think of the basic color you want for each room. White is easily the nicest color for kitchens, maybe lighter blues for bathrooms; and it's almost a joke theory, but they say shades of apricot, salmon, or orange make people feel hungry, and are ideal colors for dining rooms. It's a good starting point to gather ideas and samples for each room and later, when it comes to decision time, you can use them to start putting together a scheme.

When it comes to decisions about curtains, you should make notes about what you need practically and esthetically in each room. There are a lot of options, including no drapes at all, traditional curtains, curtains plus shades, roller blinds, Roman blinds—or just sheers, or blinds and sheers. They all do something different.

You have to think how you want the light to enter the room and how to control it. In bedrooms, you want to create an atmosphere that is softer, or more flamboyant, than elsewhere in the house. In drawing rooms and dining rooms, you might just have dress curtains. In kitchens, you don't want drapes dipping into the sink, so some kind of blind is

BELOW
Green curtains with gold fringing and serious swags and tails, hung against beige-papered walls, create a totally theatrical backdrop for the elegant furniture of this room.

BELOW RIGHT
Touches of the Alhambra are evident in the bathroom of Antony's London home, where the cutouts on the valance echo the minaret shapes of the alcoves.

more appropriate. Each room should be considered on its own merits, to give every part of the house interest and distinction.

FABRIC DEVELOPMENTS

There have been huge changes in the world of fabrics. Historically, the prominent natural fiber was wool, the second most important was linen and, much later on, cotton was developed. Later still, when sea routes from the East opened up, silk was introduced from China, followed by jute and raffia from India. In northern Europe, there was even a nettle fiber, which was like a cross between silk and linen. There was quite a choice, but there were design limitations with natural fibers. Fifty years ago, manmade fibers were dreadful, but now they have qualities of handling, durability, and strength that are even becoming superior to those of natural fibers.

We now construct new fabrics using cocktails of manmade and natural fibers. A revolution is happening here. We are about halfway through a process of being able to produce fabrics that won't fade, won't wear out, have amazing tear strength, wash easily, and hang beautifully. Basically, you will be able to do anything with them.

SOUTH AFRICAN STYLE

I have a classical townhouse in London and a country house, so in Cape Town I wanted something different. It's a Roman villa, something I've admired since I went to Pompeii. All the rooms open off a square central courtyard open to the sky. All around the outside is a 13-foot-deep covered veranda—a *stoep*. Curtaining is difficult because of the strong sunlight, but the deep *stoep* shelters the windows and keeps the rooms cool, so I've used dress curtains to give atmosphere and decoration. "

> We now construct new fabrics using cocktails of manmade and natural fibers. A revolution is happening here

TESSA KENNEDY

For more than thirty years, Tessa Kennedy has been designing imaginative and distinctive interiors for a variety of clients, both private and commercial. Her styles may be rich, colorful, and elaborate or contemporary, simple, and elegant, depending on the requirements of the commissions. Having gained a worldwide following, her recent projects include the new Rivoli bar and casino at London's Ritz Hotel; and she has designed the homes of such celebrities as Pierce Brosnan and George Harrison. Tessa has also designed the total remodeling and restoration of a number of large London houses and apartments.

Don't look to me for a minimalist job. I love layers upon layers of beautiful things. I love fabrics that are rich, such as cashmeres, silks, and velvets. Although they might be expensive at the outset, the glory of them is that they don't date and are very easy to care for.

I have been working for years in Claridges Hotel in London, and there are rooms I designed as long as twelve years ago that still look as if they were done yesterday, because they are timeless in style. You can't afford to use anything cheap if you want it to look good and last. The color of good fabrics and trimmings doesn't fade, they don't shrink, and they hang correctly.

MORE AND LESS

I love luxury and I think you should use plenty of fabric when making drapes—although you can have too much of a good thing. I had one client who insisted on oversized curtains; they were four and a half times the width of the window, and then they had three feet of fabric pooled on the ground. What a client wants a client gets, but I felt that this was claustrophobic. I don't like being skimpy either, but you have to know where to stop. I think the biggest mistake people tend to make when it comes to curtaining is to get the scale wrong. There's a middle way that's just right—and it's somewhere between too skimpy and too much.

ABOVE
An uncompromising pair of plush red velvet curtains adorns a large period room already crowded with color. The curtains take the color and interest right up to ceiling level, to chandeliers and pictures hung high on the walls.

LEFT
A detail of the curtain shows the gorgeous red tassel and bobble-edged tieback and the modern, Russian-inspired embroidered trim at the base.

RIGHT
Against the pink velvet wall, the valance hangs from an antique gilded valance board. Chenille fringing on the edges of the valance and on the leading edge and base of the curtains finishes them off to perfection.

The dining room curtains from Rudolf Nureyev's Paris flat now hang at the windows of this magnificent London bedroom. Their sweep of color frames a large window and window seat.

ABOVE LEFT

The silk tassel tiebacks of the curtains pick up on the colors used in the room. Somehow, the dramatic curtains demand tiebacks—the performance can't begin until the curtains are drawn aside.

GLOBAL INFLUENCES

Being of Slav descent, I have been very influenced by Russia and, in particular, by the Russian Ballet. Rudolph Nureyev was a great friend, and over many years I helped him with his houses, finding antiques and sourcing old fabrics. I also watched him spend hours working with his set designer and observed his interest in every tiny detail of a fabric, from how it looked when the light hit it to how it hung or draped.

I do quite a lot of work in Los Angeles. There, I am very influenced by the environment, especially the climate, the ocean, and the palm trees. I think the Southwestern look is too banal by itself. I prefer Southwest meets Mexico, because it incorporates Native American design with Mission gothic—both styles I love.

I think the traditional English curtain ensemble of valances, swags, and tails has had its day, even in stately homes. The biggest change I can see is the input of Japanese design. People no longer want masses of fabric that collects dust. They like a spare look that is still rich, with exquisite detail, and screens or blinds to diffuse light. 99

RIGHT

A dramatic tented dressing room is curtained with an exotic mixture of striped taffetas and *devoré* velvets. The entrance curtains that lead through into the bedroom are tied back high up so one can pass easily through the gap.

FAR RIGHT

A detail of the curtains in the tented room shows the trimmings and braids, which are made from sections of antique embroideries from Turkestan.

I love luxury and I think you should use plenty of fabric when making curtains—although you can have too much of a good thing

NICHOLAS HASLAM

Crisp interiors that blend traditional and contemporary design elements are Nicholas Haslam's signature. He declares that the whole point of interior design is to make people look wonderful and feel happy in their environment. His designs are influenced by a vast range of styles, except, he says, the late Victorian and Art Deco. He has created interiors for a clientele that reads like a Who's Who of rock royalty and eccentric aristocrats, with whom he works and plays. Nicholas Haslam's interior design work—always with an element of surprise—is to be found in homes throughout the world.

66 The construction of windows has changed considerably. People now accept sliding windows and expanses of plate glass that are practically invisible as structures, whereas twenty years ago everyone preferred glazing bars, Georgian panes, and the horizontal lines of sashes. Now you have to work the blank glass into your idea of what makes a beautiful view.

DESIGN

I think people have begun to think of windows as works of art. A window is like a modern painting and curtains compose the frame. When closed, the curtains have to replace the view and be beautiful in themselves. Not surprisingly, curtains have become a dirty word because of all the over-the-top ruffles and endless pools of fabric on the floor. Curtains were used to achieve a decor, to make the room, so you entered and that was all you saw. Thankfully, people have got much sharper in their expectations now, and they are beginning to see curtains as part of an integrated whole.

I often avoid curtains altogether, but when I do use them, I think they can give a room a bit of welcome height. Now that we don't always have pillars to take the eye up to the ceiling, that's a job that curtains can do. If you take them up as high as you can, they give visual height to a room and draw attention to the ceiling.

I will do lining and interlining if it needs to be done, but I don't do it automatically, because it doesn't always look right and it makes the curtains a nightmare to pull. I tend to use three layers of curtains instead of linings. For example, I'll have a couple of colored silks as inner layers, so you can choose the atmosphere, and a final layer that blocks out the light.

I use different ways of drawing curtains, such as the reef-pulls that are designed for theater curtains, which pull the fabric up and well out of the way into dramatic sculptural

ABOVE
In the hall of a house in the French quarter of New Orleans, the stairs dominate and the room needs a strong, vertical window treatment for balance. The brilliant red curtains are made from British guardsman's cloak material, edged with contrasting green grosgrain.

RIGHT
No pattern could compete with the amazing papered walls in the drawing room of the house. The drapes are plain pink silk taffeta hung over plain white sheers, but the elaborate valances, with their rosettes and tassels, echo the magnolias and curving branches on the walls.

folds. Curtains should hang just to the floor, although I am beginning
to think it could look quite chic to have them stopping a few inches
short, so they hover just above the floor.

FABRIC CHOICES

I love fabric, but not necessarily ruinously expensive silks. I like to see a
stream of color going up either side of a window to give a column-like
effect. I don't use elaborate brocades for curtains, as I prefer to use
exotic patterns on furniture, keeping the pattern down low in the room.
I like curtains made of inexpensive fabric; my absolute favorite is a
fabric by Marvic called "Renishan." It's a thick type of linen that hangs
so well, like carved folds. My favorite fabric for under curtains is called
"Eclipse." It's a metallic fabric manufactured like the lining of photo-
graphic umbrellas, so the light bounces off it. I sometimes install

lighting under the ceiling cornice so the curtains beneath glitter and
glow at night. I look at the walls and curtains together, and I'll sometimes use the same patterned fabric for both, using the reverse side for
one or the other.

I try not to use tiebacks on my curtains, because I think they are
now clichés. I don't go in for conventional trimmings, either. I tend to
use crystals, shells, leather, or cheap gaudy braid instead, but I do use
tassels, overscaled, and lots of them. If I do a valance, I like it to have
a strong, masculine shape, which I'll either have made of wood or of
fabric that, by the time I've finished with it, will look as if it's sculpted
from wood. If I use swags and tails, again I'll use them with a twist,
perhaps putting the tails upside down and with an amazing contrast
lining, so they come as a total surprise. I think surprise is the new
direction in interior design.

This bedroom in the New Orleans house was inspired by a mirror-fronted clothes closet painted with birds and sprays of flowers. The cotton fabric on the walls and the bed-curtains is printed with an eighteenth-century design that suits the room perfectly.

BELOW
A detail reveals the floral fabric used on its reverse side for the walls—to give a washed-out, faded look—and then the right way round for the bed curtains.

FORESIGHT

Modern architects put windows just where you don't want them, because they think of the outside first and then carve up the resulting space into rooms. That's why it is always vital, when looking at new build or a massive remodeling, to call in the decorator the instant the architect starts work. The most difficult windows to deal with are those that open inward and those huge Venetian windows in three arched sections, that are best left unadorned.

People are in their houses less often during the day, so rooms are much more orientated to night, and that's why I do different layers. The outer curtains, I think, are left largely undrawn. Old-fashioned curtains rather shut you in, and now people want a feeling of space—or at least the illusion of space—and you get that through a translucent layer of colored silk or the backlit glow of a metallic sheer. "

people have got much sharper in their expectations, and they are beginning to see curtains as part of an integrated whole

GABHAN O'KEEFFE

Neither Louis XIV or Ludwig of Bavaria would have felt ill-at-ease in the opulent, unsparing interiors created by this master of fantasy. An Irishman born in South Africa, Gabhan O'Keeffe is known in the decorating world as a man who paints with a broad design brush. The secret, he says, is to know precisely where the line should be drawn between grandeur and vulgarity. O'Keeffe has become something of the darling of the international glitterati, naming such luminaries as Isabel Goldsmith, Gloria Von Thurn und Taxis, and Lucy Ferry amongst his clients.

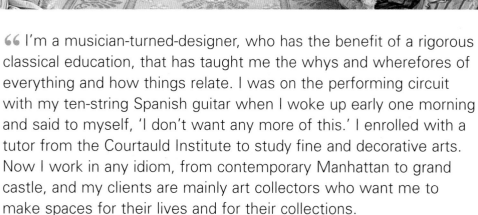

❝ I'm a musician-turned-designer, who has the benefit of a rigorous classical education, that has taught me the whys and wherefores of everything and how things relate. I was on the performing circuit with my ten-string Spanish guitar when I woke up early one morning and said to myself, 'I don't want any more of this.' I enrolled with a tutor from the Courtauld Institute to study fine and decorative arts. Now I work in any idiom, from contemporary Manhattan to grand castle, and my clients are mainly art collectors who want me to make spaces for their lives and for their collections.

LIVING WITH TEXTILES

The experience of textiles is almost your first sensual contact when you are born, and you can express yourself through the personality textiles possess. People choose their clothes in fine weaves, seductive silks, or chunky knits as self-expression. You can relate all yarns back to the physical. It's the same with a home. It should be a sensual experience of sound, feel, and the sight of colors.

OPPOSITE ABOVE

A dressing room, bedroom, and bathroom in an English country house use tenting, wall hangings, and elaborate curtains to disguise asymmetrical windows and sloping ceilings. The bed is covered with studded silk velvet and its hangings are sumptuously decorated with fringes and tassels.

OPPOSITE BELOW

In the library of an apartment in Paris, the walls are loose-hung with golden silk brocade, edged with silk Jacquard tape. The curtains are triple-layered—swagged valances of chinoiserie silk taffeta, over curtains of striped taffeta edged in cord, and under curtains of multi-colored checks.

I design the textiles and the colorways for every curtain design project I take on. In fact, I consider the development of yarns and weaving techniques to be the most important part of my work. For example, I was working recently on a viscose velvet that I wanted to be a deep saffron yellow, but I couldn't get the dye to the depth I wanted, until I experimented with an acrylic yarn instead. That's how you create new fabrics in colorways that did not exist before.

A lot of designers go to India to manufacture their fabrics, but I find that England is one of the best sources of talent for weaving and handwork. The craftspeople here have both the expertise and the sophistication that it takes to produce successful and beautiful fabrics.

WORKING WITH ARCHITECTURE

Window treatments have to engage with the architecture. For me, it's the room that dictates the texture and color of the hangings, so I don't just use fabric at windows, but also on walls and in doorways. You don't have to go the conventional route with lengths of fabric hanging meekly from a valance any more. Anything is possible, and I use textiles like a painter uses color. I like to stimulate the eye with color and create fabulous interiors that engage all the senses.”

For me, it's the room that dictates the texture and color of the hangings

ABOVE

Over an Indian rosewood bed hangs a cupola covered in faded violet velvet, decorated with pom-poms and cords. The bed hangings are of hand painted and gold-printed pleated silk. The mohair velvet closet hangings and the curtains were designed and woven specially for the room.

SERA HERSHAM LOFTUS

Born in London and brought up listening to the music of Janis Joplin and Jimi Hendrix, Sera Hersham Loftus says that she was given free expression of style from a very young age. She left school at sixteen to pursue a career as a super-stylist. After a time spent working for a number of dance companies in Israel, she moved back to London to art-direct fashion shoots and music videos, and, she says, to create super-stylish spaces for super-funky people. Her design philosophy is based on the motto that you should style your spaces as you would style yourself—to keep you real and cool at all costs.

OPPOSITE AND ABOVE
It could be a stage set, but in fact it's a drawing-room created for one of Sera's clients. The curtains are made of claret silk velvet with gold-metal embroidery. The detail shows how they hang straight and pool on the floor, and how the embroidery of the valance is repeated on the base. The crushed velvet of the curtain looks wonderful against the distressed finish of the walls.

> " A room may begin to evolve for me in a market. I'll find something charming, maybe a piece of exquisitely worn fabric. If it's something that's winked at me, then I'll use that as a starting point. Then I trawl around to find something that will go with it, which could be anything—a shawl, a footstool, an antique rose—and I'll build a room around that magpie collection. My sitting room started with a remnant of an emerald green cut-velvet shawl.

DESIGNER HOME

I use a lot of curtains, but not necessarily at windows. In my drawing room, I've used antique, handmade Japanese *sudari* blinds. They give a wonderful diffused light, look exotic, and I can see out into the garden— but no one can look in. You could get the same effect using pinoleum blinds stained a dark chocolate brown, edged with fabrics and decorated with interesting tassels and antique ribbons along the bottom. I use fabric everywhere else in the room, except for the windows. I took away the doors and put up curtains to cover the openings into the drawing room. Doors take up too much room and they're too final, so I take my curtains right up to the ceiling, to give the room a bit of scale.

Curtains make the room cozy and give it the element of mystery that I love. I use antique curtains that I pick up in markets, but if I can't find what I want and have to start from scratch, then I'll make the fabrics look old. I think colors look better when they're faded and fabrics look better when they've had the newness beaten out of them. I'll add antique lace here and there, because you can just about see through it, and it diffuses light, which adds to the feeling of mystery. I don't always put things up for practical reasons, I put them up because they're beautiful. I'd rather see beautiful curtains than cabinet doors. I hang drapes in my garden in the summer, which transforms it into a Bollywood dream.

LEFT
Sera's own bedroom changes its look constantly. On this particular day, the room was hung with pink-and-purple saris tied to wires stretched across the ceiling. Pieces of antique lace and ready-made linen curtains completed the colorful design whole.

ABOVE
Among the market finds draped about this enchanting room is a beautifully printed wedding sari, which is attached to an overhead wire with simple ties.

When I'm hunting around the markets, it's the fabrics that choose me. I love old damask silks, because they've got an elegant patina to them. I love the way old velvet hangs. If it's an old fabric with personality it'll find me, and even if it's gone a bit in places, I'll chop it up and make pillows out of it, or a lampshade. I salvage all kinds of otherwise discarded textiles, be it lingerie lace or 1930s satin corsets, to make my lampshades.

LATERAL THINKING
Decorating is about lateral thinking. It doesn't have to be the way it's always been. One thing many adults still expect is to be told how to decorate their homes. People who have grown out of this can do any-

thing they want. There's no reason why you can't use shawls as curtains, curtains as tablecloths or throws, antique linen as valances or antique sheets as curtains. Why not?

I think a home should be a place in which you immediately feel relaxed—a safe, womb-like place to be. My style is described as bohemian gypsy or *fin-de-siècle* French boudoir with a bordello chic feeling. It's eclectic, individual and pretty—very exotic and erotic. I'd really like it if my clients moved things around in their homes in the same way that I do, but when I go back six months later, a room is always the same as when I left it. My next goal is to give my clients the confidence to shuffle things around, to add, subtract, and keep their rooms fluid.

I will use a different approach in a boudoir, because you have to have darkness there, but I'm still not going the conventional route. In my children's bedrooms, for example, I put up practical white blackout blinds, which turned out to be perfect canvases for painting. Now, instead of curtains, they have funky images at their windows. I like screens, because they give a bit of mystery. I lean toward mysterious people as well, people who don't reveal all of themselves, leaving plenty of layers to get to know. It's the same with a house: you shouldn't be able to see or feel everything at once. **"**

I think colors look better when they're faded and fabrics look better when they've had the newness beaten out of them

66 I treat windows in a bold way, so that they become features, rather than something that just happened to the room. Often, you can disguise ugly architectural detailing or badly proportioned or unattractive windows with a skillful treatment. If you want an understated look, just use plain white, reverse-rolled blinds.

I make decisions about how to treat windows at the very beginning of a project, because they are the features of the room that can bring the most change. You can't treat them in isolation from the rest of the decoration. I like to oversee the entire process, if I can, from the weaving of the fabric to the making up and hanging of the curtains, because I

MICHAEL LEWIS

According to Michael Lewis, design should look effortless, concealing any complexities within. He considers interior design to be a science, rather than an art, as it is linked in an equation with budget and with the personality of the client for whom it is intended. He is a designer who is inspired by a challenge—such as a Presidential yacht in the Philippines, a beach house in California, or a Grade I listed mansion right next door to Buckingham Palace. Even low-budget commissions escape compromise. Michael Lewis will use the finest quality linen rather than poor quality silk.

don't believe in delegating visual decisions. The serendipity that occurs when hanging the curtains—the way a tail is dressed or the height and sweep of a curtain held by a tieback—can only be achieved on site. Fabric can only be draped in real life and not on a drawing board; and besides, this is the most exciting part of the design process. The window treatment as a whole combines the qualities of the curtain maker and the artfulness of the curtain fitter with the knee-jerk reaction and creativity of the designer.

I don't design ordinary things; I like to design extraordinary things that work with the client's possessions and art collections. The result has to reflect them; I don't want them to walk in at the end and see something that they can't relate to. But I do like to push them a bit, to make them reevaluate, consider new ideas and widen their visual experience and vocabulary.

ONE-OFF FABRICS

I often commission a length of textile or panel—whether *devoré*, appliqué or something custom dyed or woven—and treat the window as a set piece. It is the antithesis of the fabric-by-the-yard look and becomes a work of art in its own right. I really don't like curtains that appear to have won the competition for how many yards of fabric you can throw at a window! Curtains need to be orderly and elegant.

I have always had a passion for fabrics and there are certain geniuses whose textiles I love to work with. Jack Lenor Larsen has to be the world's number one creator, who pushes the boundaries and creates the most subtle and unusual pieces—often elaborating on traditional tribal techniques and Old World looms, but working with high-tech and unusual fibers. Ulf Moritz is following his lead, and so, too, is the Japanese company, Nuno. All produce wondrous fabrics from materials as diverse as paper, plastic, grass, and metal. Sabina Fay Braxton has developed a combination of embossed velvet panels and *devoré* for me that is very exciting. Pietro Seminelli has created origami panels for me, which are made up into Roman blinds out of abaca fibers, so you end up with two and three thicknesses of light and shadow, making a very tailored solution to elegant sheers.

GOLDEN RULES

Never skimp on the amount of fabric you use. You may decide on an inexpensive plain fabric, such as calico lining, even sheets or kitchen towels blanket-stitched together, but use a lot of it—two and a half to three times fullness is absolutely required. If you don't want to draw attention to the window, use crisp white roller blinds; and unless your ceiling is over eleven feet tall, do not consider hanging your curtains or blinds from anywhere but immediately below the cornice. Always sail the curtains way beyond the width of the window to give the illusion that your windows are wider than they actually are. Use a deep hem

LEFT

In this drawing room created for one of Michael Lewis's clients in a beautiful penthouse, the curtains are made of a classic Fortuny fabric with a white-on-white design that, apparently, was Greta Garbo's favorite. The under curtains are gold/silver crinkled metallic sheer.

FAR LEFT

A detail of the drawing room curtains shows that the fabric was used on its reverse side for the curtains and the correct side for the frilled valance. Crystals edge the curtains to catch the light; and the tassels on the valances sparkle with glass beads.

on sheers, which will give them a much more elegant and lush feel. Forget the hokum of never putting long curtains over a radiator—the heat will not merely go out the window, the radiator will actually heat up the cold air coming into the room. Vacuum your heavy drapes periodically and have your sheers cleaned regularly, as nothing is more depressing than soiled, gray sheers. Finally, get your curtains professionally made and make sure that they are long enough; if necessary, use leaded weights in the bottom hem to help them hang properly. "

> I don't design ordinary things; I like to design extraordinary things that work with the client's possessions and art collections

Michael Lewis

ABOVE

In an Arts and Crafts inspired London home, Michael Lewis has created an end-wall of curtain that cannot be ignored. A deep smock-headed valance hangs from a heavy timber pole, arching and dipping over the window. Dark blinds are electronically controlled to block out the light when required.

RIGHT

The large plaid curtains have deep tassel fringes and tassel and rope tiebacks. The curtains are perfectly made and pleated so that each fold shows one color. These are serious curtains that fulfill Lewis's ambition to "design extraordinary things."

BELOW

A totally stunning dining room with a molded silver ceiling and a shimmering cornice has a pair of purple damask curtains edged with crystal drops. The room sparkles to create a suitable environment for the magnificent Patrice Butler crystal-and-amethyst chandelier.

RIGHT

Crystal chandelier drops also hang along the leading edge of the curtains, and even the tiebacks are made of silvery mauve thread. The dramatic sheers are of silver organza edged with glass beads.

AMAL & PERIHAN AL-UZRI

Amal Al-Uzri was born and trained as a designer in Lebanon. A subsequent move to London gave her a new perspective on interior design, which she then took with her when she moved with her family to Bahrain. There she developed a reputation that led to design commissions from international bankers and from the Bahraini royal family. Recently, she formed her company AAU Designs back in London. Her daughter Perihan Al-Uzri comes to design from much the same classical tradition as her mother, adding to it a contemporary imagination and a keen eye for detail and for exciting new materials.

ABOVE LEFT AND RIGHT
In this bright, sun-filled drawing room, the beautifully made taffeta dress curtains are lined and inter-lined, draped, swagged, tailed, and pleated to perfection, and then fringed and braided to show off their elegant lines. This is a room that is the epitome of elegance. Exquisite furniture and works of art need an exquisite showcase.

OPPOSITE AND ABOVE CENTER
A lovely, asymmetrical, draped curtain, reminiscent of the simple Regency look, hangs under the elaborately carved cornice that runs all around the ceiling of this magnificent drawing room. The silk curtains are perfectly pleated and edged with a heavy gold fringe to accentuate their shape. The sheers are of antique lace. Amal has added her own exquisite touches here with dramatic stripy ropes reminiscent of gondoliers' poles and hangings of gold fabric to brighten up the corner of the room. All the fixings and tracks are neatly hidden by the chunky cornice.

66 It is important that homes not only look beautiful, but that they are also comfortable. We use our imagination to make thematic spaces to enrich our clients' lives and make their dreams come true.

AMAL AL-UZRI

I feel that my Middle Eastern background and exposure to the West from my base in London allow me to marry the two cultures in my design work. Windows are of great importance to me. I like to dress a window in the same way that a couturier dresses a woman—to hide the flaws and emphasize the best characteristics.

The choice of fabric and cut for curtains is dictated by the theme of the room. I love fabulous silks and hand-embroidery. Although these are the fabrics you expect to find in palaces, you don't need to use expensive fabric to make a beautiful window. The biggest change I have noticed in the twenty-first century is to accessories. There is now so much available on the market to provide detailing. I would never economize on the detailing or on the cut of a pair of curtains.

PERIHAN AL-UZRI

My mother's approach to decorating is very classical, and I come from the same starting point. When thinking about design, you have to consider the existing architecture and style of the window. The style of the curtain very much depends on the room and its function. Because I use a variety of styles and fabrics, the end result is entirely different. I prefer plain fabrics and like rough, natural textures, such as linen. I also like contrast—a leather valance and leather tiebacks on sheer curtains, or bamboo blinds bordered in silk.

The wide range of fabrics now available on the market—such as jute, embroidered suede, laser-cut sheers, or crystal-beaded fabrics—stretches the design imagination. Any one of these fabrics can be the start of a new story in design. Just about anything you can dream up is technically possible, which is why interior design is so exciting and moving in a different direction now. 99

I feel that my Middle Eastern background and exposure to the West from my base in London allow me to marry the two cultures

LEFT
Alidad's signature look is the dark, womb-like interior where patterns pile on patterns, and this wonderful sitting room is typical. The pattern is concentrated all over the walls, on table tops and pillows, but the sofa and curtains are plain.

RIGHT
Mimmi O'Connell, whose work is featured in the Simple section, also turns her hand to the dramatic. This classically proportioned room is an absolute riot of patterns, and there isn't a surface that's not crammed with lovely things.

FAR RIGHT
Another stunning room by Mimmi displays multiple layers of fabric tied and twisted to show off their underskirts. This is way beyond the style you would expect in a Georgian interior—it's a modern, ironic take on the traditional swag-and-tieback routine.

BELOW RIGHT
Panels of dramatic, Egyptian-style fabric hang around the perimeter of this beautifully proportioned traditional window. The original shutters can be used to exclude the light and a simple sheer blind is there to filter it.

DRAMATIC ENDINGS

Add a theatrical touch, a flamboyant streak, and a sense of fun to a thorough grounding in the decorative arts and you get dramatic style. All these designers were chasing atmosphere. Some found it by placing pattern upon pattern, some developed it with rich, expensive fabrics, and others created it with an abundance of inexpensive linen sculpted into dramatic folds. Whatever route they use to achieve their aims, they all share an ability to create highly individual rooms.

We saw Amal Al-Uzri take her own sense of the dramatic to perhaps its ultimate conclusion—the creation of a fictional setting. "We use our imagination and skill to make thematic spaces to enrich the lives of women whose only perspective is the home," she explains. "We make rooms to dream in, rooms that will transport our clients to China or to Venice, to Paris or to a Moroccan bazaar." Sera Hersham Loftus described her style as exotic and erotic, one that intends to be mysterious; and Michael Lewis summed it up for me when he said that he liked to design "extraordinary things."

BEYOND FASHION

One of the serendipitous consequences of going for the extraordinary is that the room will never be either in fashion or out of it. This

sense of the unique is often achieved through the design of curtains, when imagination takes full flight. Both Gabhan O'Keeffe and Sera Hersham Loftus use fabric wherever they possibly can. Sera uses curtains "everywhere in the room except for covering up the windows" and Gabhan uses fabric "not just at windows but on walls and in doorways." These are designers who extend the very definition of a curtain, placing it way beyond the confines of a window treatment.

As well as the designers whose master classes feature here, I also spoke to Alidad in London, whose signature look is a dark, womb-like interior. I discovered that curtains were a very important component of his style. "My rooms have warm colors, fabrics piled one on top of the other, and that is the sort of room that requires curtains," he states. "The curtains are the last layers that you wrap around the room to make it a place you feel safe in."

The last word on the dramatic style, though, has to go to Nicholas Haslam, who works to produce beautifully made curtains that come as a total surprise. Using unconventional trimmings, over-scaled elements, and amazing contrasting linings, nothing about his designs is predictable. "Surprise," says Nicholas, "is the new direction." His work here, and that of the other dramatic designers, is certainly testament to this idea.

There is a significant move in contemporary design toward an elegant, **tailored look** that is as much about what to leave out of the equation as what to put in. When I interviewed the designers featured here, I found that for each of them, the architecture was of paramount importance. More often than not, they used drapes as an extension of the architecture of a room, blending them imperceptibly with the walls. This is a style that is calm, but remains beautiful and very chic. I would further define it as cool and understated without the starkness of minimalism. It is definitely an **urban style**, and rooms decorated in this way have a special stillness about them, a feeling that probably emanates from the perfection of the tailoring and the visible attention to detail that is lavished upon them by their makers.

The tailoring analogy was used a great deal by the designers I interviewed. Many people talked of curtain making, and soft furnishings in general, in terms of *haute couture*, and I think that is what epitomizes this style for me. It's like an Armani suit, **perfectly cut**, exquisitely stitched, and of wonderful textiles that breathe and hang. These designers use every trick in the fabric technology handbook to create stunning effects. They create perfect backdrops for art without overwhelming it, creating urban havens of **exquisite taste**. Whether it's a collection of Old Masters or Abstract Expressionists, this is a style that shows an understanding that it is the collection that needs displaying, not the style itself. That is probably why so many collectors turn to designers working in this field to create interiors for them.

One of the other features that distinguishes tailored design from minimalism is the use of color. Well-judged slabs of vibrant color that give a room a subtle personality are carefully devised by tailored designers, where minimalists might hesitate to use bright color at all. All these designers were able to draw on diverse aspects of design to achieve the smartest looks. I found that they approached each project looking firmly toward the future but knowing what not to reject from the past.

ailored

NANCY BRAITHWAITE

A graduate of Michigan State University, Nancy Braithwaite began her design career as the first female industrial designer for the Sunbeam Corporation. In 1969, while living in New York, she launched Nancy Braithwaite Interiors, which is now located in Atlanta, Georgia. The company designs private residential interiors and projects for museums and exhibitions, using both traditional and contemporary design ideas. Nancy Braithwaite's work appears frequently in influential magazines, such as *House Beautiful* and *Town and Country*.

LEFT
Magnificent floor-to-ceiling windows with strong architectural lines get just a whisper of a gauzy sheer hung from an almost invisible pole. The windows are overlooked only by a garden, so it is all they need.

RIGHT
Smart brown and cream silk stripes hang straight from a strong horizontal track. The curtains hang softly to the floor like an elegant couture ballgown, giving the sculptural room a soft touch.

FAR RIGHT
A wonderful room, dominated by tall French windows on all sides, has no wall space for art or decoration. These beautifully made, full-length curtains give the room all the decoration it needs. Dark blue Roman blinds are parked way up above the window

❝ It's very simple: a window is part of a wall which, in turn, is part of the architecture of the room. I try to add to the architecture of a room, and I look at architecture in a broad sense. It's not just a space enclosed by four walls, it can include the furniture within it. So the first question I ask myself is how I can improve on what's already here and ensure the windows enhance the character of the room.

If the windows are dumpy and ugly, then they're going to need help; if they're fabulous, they can be left alone. I don't dive in there to bury a window under a heap of swirls and twirls. For me, it's important to respect the integrity of a window as a light source and a view of the world.

DRESSING

I don't go into a room with any preconceived ideas; my mind is open. I treat each window individually and as a group within the room. If it's a great light source, there's a great view and privacy isn't an issue then, if possible, I won't cover it up. Any treatment will cover parts of the window, and to drape it with valances would foreshorten it, slam it down. Verticality is my rule. All windows should have that tall, elegant, slender feeling, like a well-dressed person. I think curtains are like

clothes for a window, they should be flattering. So if you're faced with a sad, ugly window, you've got to try and help out. With good tailoring, short and fat can become tall and thin, and it's the same for windows. You've got the whole of the wall to play with, so you can always do something to give a window height. You can slenderize with vertical columns of fabric either side. You deal with each window as it affects the room.

My curtains, my draperies, don't smother; they change the badly proportioned and enhance the beautifully proportioned. I suppose it is significant that I have no curtains in my own home, because I don't need them. I have custom-made shutters. My home is architecturally what it needs to be. It's a New England farmhouse, very simple, and I don't think curtains would help; it's perfectly beautiful as it is.

ABOVE LEFT

Softly pleated curtains in shades of pale gold and black encircle this room, leaving the lovely, tall sash windows unencumbered. The geometry of the glazing bars has a calm, zen-like quality that is a decoration in itself.

TOP RIGHT

Nancy has dressed these windows as if they were going somewhere elegant for dinner. The folds are impeccable and the matching Roman blind acts as a visual valance, bringing the height of the room down to cozier proportions.

ABOVE RIGHT

Lovely paneling deserves to be shown off. In this room, curtains would dominate and hide too much, so stylish, opaque white Roman blinds have just the required degree of softness.

STARTING POINTS

First you have to look at the house, consult with the client and find out their needs for privacy, light, fresh air, and views. Then you decide how you're going to treat the window. Are you going to do nothing at all, go for a see-through scrim—you can do amazing things with simple materials—or for the heavy lined and interlined look?

I'm not a chintz lady. I usually do not use pattern, because when you gather it up it becomes meaningless, except in very unusual cases. I prefer to work with texture and color. I love lightweight fabric and very heavy fabric, and I don't like anything in between. When I do floating draperies I leave then unlined so the light comes through, or I'll use heavy bulk lining in the Colefax & Fowler style.

INFLUENCES

All my jobs look totally different from one another. You would not know they were mine, except by recognizing the calm, the quietness, and the color work. I don't like clutter, that's a basic, because I don't understand the need for it. I keep coming back to the analogy of the design of clothes. If you put on a beautifully cut, black dress, and then you start loading on jewelry and accessories, pretty soon you don't know what you're supposed to be looking at. It's too busy; you've lost the focus. It's the same with draperies—I'm tired of fringes and trimmings. I'm more interested in constructing draperies like a dressmaker, with a dressmaker's detail. Draperies should be strong enough to stand on their own, without the help of tricks.

A delightful, witty bedroom is typical of Nancy's style. The heading at the top of the bed curtains is of the same coarse linen and cut to the same depth as the valances that decorate the tops of the windows and hide the practical shades.

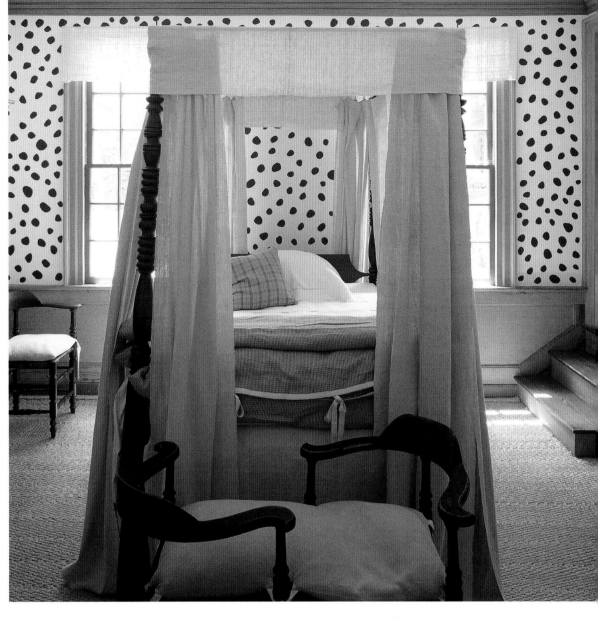

If you look at the work of great designers, you see that it has strength, simplicity, quietness, and a purity of form, whether it's drapery, furniture, or clothing. As for heroes, anything that Mr. Armani does is okay with me. I think he understands how to dress a woman, how to drape a woman. There are no tricks about it. Calvin Klein works in the same way. They both get down to the essence of a beautiful piece of fabric that is beautifully cut. That's how a pair of curtains should be.

My style is always evolving and I hope I'm getting better at what I do. It depends a lot on the clients. If they understand what you're doing, if they can see what you see, then you can bring your best to the table. Working with a nervous client is very restricting for a designer.

THE FUTURE

I love to drape beds. I think the bed is the most important part of the bedroom and I love to fulfill the fantasy. I use a lot of fabric to get the vertical feeling going. I'm doing headboards now which are nine feet tall. I just want to pull the eye up all the time. I love overscale, and I don't mean what we consider "bad taste Californian big." I like things to be just a little taller than you think they should be, just a little bigger than you think they should be. That in-between ordinary scale doesn't interest me at all any more. Little is great and big is great.

To a large extent, most people are much happier with a more typical, safe, romantic look. But I hope the general idea of what constitutes good taste is becoming simpler. But then what's good and what's bad when it comes to taste? It's totally subjective, and in the end it's personal style that counts. 99

I prefer to work with texture and color. I love lightweight fabric and very heavy fabric, and I don't like anything in-between

FRÉDÉRIC MÉCHICHE

An early interest in architecture and decorative style, and meetings with many original design minds, resulted in Frédéric Méchiche undertaking major design projects, even while he was a student. He is unafraid to mix period furniture, ancient works of art, and contemporary objects in the same interior. He is also a designer keenly aware of the practical demands of a home, such as climate, light, and color tones. A perfectionist who insists on overseeing all aspects of a design, he travels widely—for example, between a penthouse in Caracas, an English country house, and a hotel in Paris, where he is based.

LEFT
This curtain is in a wonderfully elaborate room with grey/green and gold cornicing and plasterwork, so it has to be simple—an egg-plant-colored fabric with a feint grey/green stripe hangs from a gilded pole.

RIGHT
An entrance hall with a striking checkerboard floor gets a welcoming shot of color from this vivid green Roman blind of unlined silk. It is bordered at both the top and bottom, and vertically down the lines of ring pulls, with a smart Greek key-pattern braid.

BELOW
The pristine pleats of these utterly simple, gold silk dress curtains frame a French window. A blind of slender strips of bamboo adds an element of texture to the design and filters light softly.

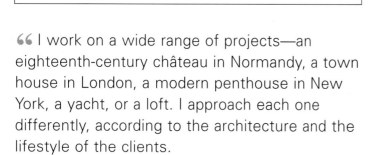

❝ I work on a wide range of projects—an eighteenth-century château in Normandy, a town house in London, a modern penthouse in New York, a yacht, or a loft. I approach each one differently, according to the architecture and the lifestyle of the clients.

The first thing to get right is the skeleton of the house, the light; the flow of space; the floors, ceilings, and walls. Once you've got a good base, all the rest can be changed to suit the mood. Many of my clients are art collectors and they come to me because they know I don't use art as decoration, I create a real home both for the art and for the people.

STYLE AND QUALITY

The curtains are elements of change in a room. When you vary the fabric or the style of upholstery or drapes, you change the atmosphere of a room; you can go from classic to modern and the place is transformed. When I do a classic interior, I never do a historic pastiche, because the result is boring, dusty, and stultifying. Often people do grand and elaborate nineteenth-century drapery in a traditional interior, but it very often turns out to be a stylistic mistake. I have seen bedrooms in some châteaux with wonderfully elaborate canopy beds *à la Polonaise* and the curtains are very simple, hung on an iron rod, which is quite correct.

For me, it is very important that curtains are beautifully made, handmade. Whether the material is expensive silk velvet or simple canvas, all my headings are handmade. My favorites are classical goblet headings, very tall and thin. I use valances very rarely; sometimes I may use a soft drape or a 1940s style, which I then cover with plaster so it looks architectural.

I like to make an interior look fresh and surprising, but have respect for tradition. I do my homework, checking the architectural details of historic homes; but then I like to absorb that elegance and atmosphere and do something different with it. Recently, I did a very pure, minimalist bedroom with curtains in luxurious white cashmere with leather binding. It's the details that are important. If you want to give an impression of comfort in a simple interior, you need a work of art, a beautiful fabric, or an amazing piece of furniture. It's about the way the elements are mixed and balanced—the simplest of white curtains in the same room as an eighteenth-century gilded chair, a totally stark interior with an amazing fabric at the window. It's like *haute couture*; there's no cheap way to do it. One half-inch either way and it's wrong. If there is a precious fabric in the room—say, a wonderful piece of embroidery—you don't need to trim it at all.

I confess to having no curtains in my own home. In my bedroom and bathroom I have simple, white canvas blackout blinds. I have too

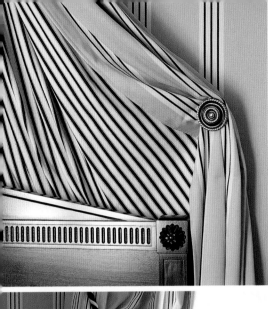

much art at home, too many photographs and too much sculpture for the distraction of curtains. I'm even moving out the furniture and the carpets in pursuit of balance.

CHANGING DIRECTION

When changing a curtain in an existing scheme, I won't do anything too drastic, because you have to add and subtract little by little to keep the balance. Fifteen years ago, I did a classical apartment in a very traditional way, with lovely antiques and elaborate silk curtains, but the client's art collection started to go in another direction—toward contemporary art—and there was too much contrast. The apartment was classically elegant with lovely proportions, beautiful paneling, and parquet flooring. I changed the silk curtains for handmade white canvas with bamboo blinds underneath, which I banded with white cotton. The Aubusson carpet was moved to another room and substituted with simple sea-grass matting. The sofa was classical eighteenth-century, and I changed the traditional upholstery fabric for white. It was still an elegant Paris apartment, but a perfect showcase for modern art. 99

ABOVE RIGHT

Cotton ticking is a wonderfully versatile fabric that comes in a variety of striped patterns and colorways. This Regency-style bedroom shows how elegant an inexpensive fabric can look when handled with aplomb.

TOP LEFT

A detail of the bed curtaining reveals blue-and-white ticking on the walls and on the bed canopy, which Méchiche has lined with an elegant dark blue-and-white stripe.

ABOVE LEFT

The detail here is of the blue-and-white ticking dress curtains that hang over simple sheers. The silk rope tieback adds another level of decoration to this beautifully coordinated room.

When you vary the fabric or the style of upholstery or curtains, you change the atmosphere of a room; you can go from classic to modern and the place is transformed

F Mechiche

LARS BOLANDER

Born and educated in Sweden, Lars Bolander is a graduate of the Stockholm and Carl Malmsten Schools of Art. He spent fifteen years in London, working for the design company Gaby Schreiber & Associates, before collaborating with Gunter Sachs on projects throughout Europe. He has lived in the United States for the past twenty years, bringing a particularly Scandinavian sensibility to his design work. He divides his time between his interior design practice and antique shop in Palm Beach, Florida and his second shop in East Hampton, New York.

ABOVE RIGHT
The lightly-lined silk taffeta curtains in this traditional library hang simply and almost straight from a slotted heading on a pole. The sheer under curtains have a separate tieback, so they can be draped independently.

RIGHT
This room has interesting proportions in its chimney breast and beams. As the wall flanking the fireplace is a seating area, obviously long curtains were not an option. Roman blinds do the job admirably.

" I like to create interiors with a touch of drama, one that might not be evident to the eye, but that is only just sensed when you first enter the room. Curtains are very important in an interior scheme, because either they can work to add a touch of theater to a room, or they can act as a more subdued element, which plays a part in the overall magic.

ANATOMY OF DRAMA

A curtain can play a role in the interior drama in several ways. The colors, the materials, and the style of curtains can all be emphasized individually and to different effect. Before deciding on curtain details, I always evaluate the existing conditions, which are unique for every design project. The natural light is different in every space, time and season, so I always try to present fabrics and colors at the location of the project if possible.

I much prefer muted color schemes, but the sensible use of a vibrant color on curtains can create a great effect. Silk taffeta is a wonderful fabric for this purpose. The material has great depth and shade variety, which adds an extra dimension to the curtains. If the rest of the room is pale, you mustn't be afraid to use bold color on the curtains, and with silk taffeta it is difficult to go wrong.

FABRIC SELECTION

I am very selective with the materials I use and the ways in which they are combined in an interior scheme. Each fabric has its own

THIS PAGE

A beautiful pair of bedroom
curtains has been padded, quilted,
and upholstered to look almost like
comforters. The effect is both
stunning and totally enveloping.
Shades do all the practical work of
keeping out light.

In this pretty dining room, the Scandinavian folk look is established by the architecture. Unlined curtains in Lars' signature muted colors hang from metal rods, and the tiebacks are accurately placed at windowsill level.

The charming scoop holding back the curtain in the dining room is a custom-made, folksy metal heart that echoes the cut-outs on the backs of the dining chairs.

wonderful qualities that need to be acknowledged. For bedroom curtains, I like to quilt plain cotton fabrics to create a feeling of warmth and coziness. Such thick curtains are best used with a pocket-heading, adding further to the relaxed look. In warmer climates, I use unlined curtains to add a flowing movement without obstructing the natural light. A stunning effect is created by using rough, heavy materials, such as burlap or raw silk.

When selecting the curtain materials, it is important not to forget the appearance of the back of the curtains. White lining is not very interesting; instead, I line curtains with checkered or striped fabrics. Ian Mankin has terrific ticking stripes in a wide variety of colors; and Chelsea Textiles is a favorite source for other stripes and checks. I also use layers of curtains for practical reasons and to create drama. Under curtains need not be plain white; and sheer fabrics are available in colorful checks and stripes.

DESIGN QUALITY

It is important to me to bring out the quality of the fabric and the beauty of its colors and patterns. I think this is best accomplished by avoiding elaborate curtain designs. Instead, I focus on details that are less obvious, but bring out the best in the fabrics. A thin interlining in silk curtains will add body and movement, qualities that are emphasized by letting the curtains sit a few inches on the floor. When you pick up the curtains and let them fall naturally, the dramatic effect is achieved.

The header should be kept simple. I like to use contrasts. A less-than-elegant header looks terrific with silk curtains, for example. Linen curtains look best with a simple, pinched pleat. If the curtains are interlined, the header should be as well, to give a less tailored look.

As an international decorator, I have had the pleasure of working with many talented artisans and craftspeople, each with a different interpretation of what is needed to achieve a unique style. When working on a project in Greece, I met a talented curtain maker whose extraordinary attention to detail was not only evident in the workmanship, but also in the presentation of proposed curtain designs. I now continue to draw from her techniques. When introducing curtain suggestions to clients, I show the fabrics hanging from actual poles, allowing a change of pole materials and styles. This gives my clients the opportunity to see how the curtain will really be, rather than having to visualize the style.

I am often asked to be involved in the development of architectural details and the interior design of a project. Recently, I completed work on a home in the Caribbean that required a total renovation inside and out. My goal was to create a union between the house and the environment. All of the small, oddly-shaped windows original to the house were replaced with French doors that opened up the interior to the exterior. Paying respect to the increase in natural light, I selected natural, lightweight fabrics and simple iron poles to frame the views.

Curtains can open any window or door to the whole world of decorating. Take an ordinary room that has no window treatment, then give it curtains, and suddenly it becomes a work of art. 99

BELOW RIGHT
The window end of the drawing room in the same house features curtains that are full length, to frame the windows and furniture and provide vertical visual impact.

BELOW LEFT
A detail of the quilted cotton curtains in the drawing room shows their stylish rope tiebacks at windowsill level. They are lined with a yellow and white Chelsea Textiles check, which has also been used on the walls.

A thin interlining in silk curtains will add body and movement, qualities that are emphasized by letting the curtains sit a few inches on the floor

JAMIE DRAKE

After more than twenty years as a designer, Jamie Drake, who works out of New York, has become renowned for creating strikingly glamorous interiors. He is also known for his ability to reflect his client's personality in each job, combining luxury and practicality in dramatic settings. His work, under the auspices of his company Drake Design Associates, has appeared in *Elle Decor*, *The New York Times*, and *House Beautiful*, among others. *Vanity Fair* described him as a "standout among the rising stars of thirty-something interior designers." He has received a string of design honors, and can name such stars as Madonna amongst his clients.

❝ I start with the proportions of a window and go from there. Often I wish windows were larger, so I design window treatments that create a bigger or elongated view instead of one that is short and squat. You can improve window proportions with curtains, and I like them to flow and breathe, to imply height. I think it's my cardinal rule—stand tall, stress the vertical, bring the eye toward the ceiling and the moldings.

ABOVE
Striking zebra patterns dominate this New York bedroom, for which Jamie Drake has chosen a vibrant yellow for the walls and the deep-dyed silk curtains. Like all the curtains in this apartment, they hang straight and are valance-free.

RIGHT
This bedroom is full of warm tobacco shades, interesting textures and patterns. The curtains are an exquisite fall of turquoise silk, bordered with gold braid. The shirred Roman blinds take up the texture story.

FABRICS OLD AND NEW

I think the greatest influence on interior design today is the technology behind certain fabrics. While I am dedicated to silk, more often I find myself drawn to metallic meshes or sheers woven with fiberglass. Metallicized fabrics are genius. Their ability to reflect the changes in natural light, dawn to dusk, dark or bright, can be quite stunning. Earth tones such as gunmetal or a deep bronze work best; the way they shimmer and reflect light is magic. A colleague of mine recently used the same fashion chain mail as Versace, but for Roman blinds. Apparently, it's not expensive and is very easy to work with. Look beyond ordinary sample books for inspiration—the possibilities are endless.

However, I love silk, truly a passionate fabric. There is no other material that can take the saturation of color that silk can and I am dedicated to color. Silks translate so wonderfully and they age so gracefully, always carrying that aura of important beauty. In the living room and dining room of my New York apartment, I have 180 yards of custom-woven Thai silk, dyed to my specifications. Nothing makes me happier than the luxury of yards and yards of fabric. But with silk it's always best to line and interline your window treatment. If I had left my curtains unlined, it would be divine to have the air wafting through, but in three years' time I'd be taking them to be rewoven as a result of the way light levels change.

I generally prefer plain fabrics, because I rely on sensational colors and textures for impact. I seldom use a pattern, but I often use contrasting borders. One of my favorite ideas is to use borders

of the same fabric but in different colors to create an accent yet retain the continuity of texture. Or I deliberately set up contrasts of texture. For example, I will use an unlined linen against a rich cotton velvet.

DRAMA AND RESTRAINT

Clients often think that if they have a post-card view, why bother with a window treatment? But a window treatment completes a room, and I encourage clients to do it before they choose their major furnishings. I would say that ninety percent of the window treatments we design are never drawn. I also

spend a lot of time advising clients to address the issue of outside lighting, so there is something to look at once the sun has set. There is nothing worse then entering a room at night and staring at a black, empty window. It removes the energy from the room and, above all, a lively spirit is the true heart to any home.

It's important never to neglect the value of your windows. They make a statement. I love the look of wood Venetian blinds, for instance. Plantation shutters can take an ordinary aluminum casement window and turn it into a finely crafted portal. Not to mention

ABOVE
The wild purple furniture and shocking pink lampshades here need a neutral background. Columns of pleated taupe silk hang straight against the walls, their fixings hidden behind a custom-built cornice.

LEFT
Vibrant fuchsia purple walls and woodwork are the backdrop for a room that is virtually pattern-free and dominated by a series of colored bar code prints. The subtle, wavy black design on the purple curtains breaks up the expanse of plain and intense color.

that an open-weave netting on a boxed shade will not only make light dance, but will also filter out harmful UV rays.

The majority of my curtains hang straight, although certain projects dictate otherwise. In bedrooms, I tend to use cornices or valances, as they help block out early morning light. On a historical project I recently completed for New York Mayor Michael R. Bloomberg, the house itself gave little room for whimsy. Gracie Mansion, the two-hundred-year-old residence of the mayors of New York, required period-style draperies—in this case, it was Federal style. At the opposite end of the spectrum, I've also done a curtain with a fringe of alternating crystal beads and found sea shells to bring a taste of the seashore to city-bound clients. 99

Metallicized fabrics are genius. Their ability to reflect the changes in natural light, dawn to dusk, can be quite stunning

ABOVE
In this bedroom, a swathe of gray silk is beautifully swagged over a simple pole framing the window. A lovely padded and quilted silk Roman blind complements the cosy, padded bedcover.

LEFT
Red, brown, and gold are the dominant colors in this drawing room designed by Jamie for a client in New York. The curtain treatment at the large windows blends with the walls—a cream silk, bordered top, bottom and leading edge in gold self-stripe satin.

SUZY CLÉ

Suzy Clé, pictured here with partner Koen, with whom she heads the design company Trendson Intérieur, has her base in a seventeenth-century house in Mechelen (Malines), Belgium. The whole interior of the house has been redesigned as a showcase for Trendson's decorating principles and taste. Her design ideas are driven by intuition and influenced by the Far East. She likes to mix European styles with exotic elements in harmonious interpretations of the two cultures. Suzy Clé has a perfectionist's eye for detail and a love of fabrics, whether classic silk damask or transparent linen.

❝ Boldness in interior design is quite rare in Belgium, but we like to shake ideas up and inspire people to do something different. There's a trend here toward large, open-plan living spaces decorated in calm, neutral colors, but the colors we like are oxblood reds, eggplant, and black.

INSPIRATIONS

We like to mix European styles with exotic elements, bringing together different cultures with a harmony that is both surprising and comfortable. We are very much influenced by the Moorish style—a kind of Spanish and North African influence that is both vibrant and eclectic.

For us, inspiration for a room can come from anywhere. Our living room, in which the walls are lined with black silk, was inspired by some prints we bought in Paris. Other rooms have been inspired by swatches of fabric, even collections of books. We are always combing through books and magazines for ideas, and while I would not call our work a reaction to minimalism—because if a client wants a modern, understated space, we are very happy to create that—our own taste is for the rich and flamboyant.

Like our furniture, which is all new rather than antique, our curtains have a traditional

Koen and Suzy Van Gestel Clé have turned their seventeenth-century home in Mechelen (Malines), Belgium into a showroom. In their drawing room, the perfect geometry of the elegant windows is complemented with elegant smokey blue-gray drapes, tied back over softly gathered, patterned shades.

LEFT
A detail of the curtains and under curtains, each held back at a different height, reveals that the silk under curtains are edged with an exquisite silk braid.

basis to their design, but we never take any-thing for granted. We'll look at a window with a fresh eye, backed up with a vast historical knowledge and the intuition that comes from working in a family decoration business that has been flourishing for seventy-five years.

I would advise against being influenced by fashion. A lot of people play too safe with their homes and take too much notice of fashion, which is quite fickle. As far as curtain treatments go, the past couple of decades have seen overblown frills, bold prints, and massive curtains puddled on the floor; then it was minimalist white roller blinds. Our philos-ophy is to work harder to create a room that is timeless, and therefore beyond fashion.

FABRICS

We are both intrigued by fabrics, and we use them not just on furniture and at windows, but wherever we like, wherever we feel a dramatic swathe of color or texture is need-ed. We will use printed fabrics, often with archive designs, and we love using classic silk damasks and brocades or very rough nat-ural materials, such as raffia or jute, for roller

ABOVE LEFT

A bright and sunny morning room in the Van Gestel Clé home has two layers of curtain hanging straight from the ceiling, with three strong lines of braiding at the bottom of the over curtains, to add interest.

ABOVE RIGHT

The morning room inner curtains are made from a checkered fabric edged with a colorful bobble trim. The shades that filter the light are made from a hand embroidered linen by Chelsea Textiles.

blinds or awnings. For curtains that are going to hang at windows we'll often use transparent linen or simple striped cotton, because you want the light to flood into a room, not to hide behind heavy drapes.

We don't use synthetic fabrics, because we believe in giving what some people might think of as old-fashioned fabrics a new lease on life. In the environments that we create, these fabrics suddenly become interesting; they create curiosity.

We mix patterns together, textures with plains, which is quite risky, but when you get it right—and we are very persistent and painstaking—what you get is a unique space. And that's what people like in our work. "

I wouldn't call our work a reaction to minimalism—because if a client wants a modern, understated space, we are very happy to create that—but our own taste is for the rich and flamboyant

LEFT
The library/dining-room in Bill Blass's New York apartment was the epitome of smart. The cream French-pleated curtains fit into the reveals, because there is no wall to park them on. As this room is mainly used at night, the restriction of daylight is not a problem.

RIGHT
These vertical curtains, designed by Celeste Cooper for Repertoire, are made from a "leather" weave fabric; the narrow silk pelmet has strips of leather criss-crossing over it. There are a lot of straight lines and simple shapes in this drawing room, and the curtains add color and softness to the whole. At the windows, roller blinds pull up from the bottom to provide privacy.

BELOW
The white-on-white drawing room of interior designer Stephen Ryan's London home is dominated by a head of David on a plinth in front of a large picture window. This is curtained with a heavy festoon blind, ornamented with tassels.

A TAILORED FIT

Most of the designers in this section would agree with Nancy Braithwaite, who says, quite simply, "verticality is my rule. All windows should have that tall, elegant and slender feeling, like a well-dressed person." Beautiful outfits benefit from beautiful fabrics, and I think it is the meticulous way of handling color, pattern, and texture that distinguishes the tailored curtain from the rest.

A BALANCED STYLE

Frédéric Méchiche believes the style is about the balance between the simple and the extraordinary—he favors "the simplest of white curtains in the same room as an eighteenth-century gilded chair or a totally stark interior with an amazing fabric at the window." Frédéric has made what sounds like the ultimate in stylish curtains out of white cashmere with a leather binding. Suzy Clé at Trendson likes to use classic silk damasks and brocades "because we believe in giving what some people might think of as

LEFT

A bold use of contrasting bindings on the leading edge and hem, and for the tiebacks, has turned this pair of full-length curtains into a geometric work of art. It is the perfect backdrop for the clean, geometrical lines of the furnishings.

old-fashioned fabrics a new lease on life." Jamie Drake is excited by "an amazing range of metallic woven meshes and interesting sheers," but his first love is still plain silk, custom-dyed to intense color. Lars Bolander sees a move away from heavy fabrics toward flowing curtains with thin linings. Lars uses a lot of ticking, inexpensive quilted cottons, and unlined taffeta that does wonderful things with light. Like the majority of designers working in this style, Lars prefers plains to patterns, keeping checks and stripes for lining materials.

Valances, swags, and tiebacks are not a feature of this style. Where a valance is necessary, it will either be softly draped or made in simple style from wood. Windows will enjoy the slenderizing effect of vertical columns of fabric falling on either side. Whatever the fabric, the smart curtain does not smother. There will be no fringes, trimmings, or clutter, just a sense of calm, strength, and simplicity—an overriding purity of form.

Country style is one of the hardest looks to define, because it has different meanings in different countries. In the UK, for instance, country does not mean rural cottage, but a grand, **slightly eccentric** style that conjures up images of overstuffed sofas, faded carpets on stone-flagged floors, soft floral curtain fabrics, slightly scruffy but beautiful antiques, and open log fires. In America, the English country style is as comfortable, but a great deal grander and more formal, with coordinating fabrics, fat pillows, and lots of gleaming mahogany.

To add to the confusion, the American version as interpreted and redefined by American decorators, such as the late and legendary Sister Parish, has been re-exported around the world. It is in demand as a style of its own, with English people calling in American decorators to achieve the look!

Indigenous American country is another thing entirely—a style that embraces a range of wonderfully **easy-going** styles. On the East coast, the style is characterized by Cape Cod beach clapboard and shutters, driftwood, and clean crisp colors— blue-and-white with faded touches of sea-green and gray in light, billowing curtains, for example. In the American West, though, country becomes a riot of strong colors and chunky, natural shapes, incorporating bold geometric rugs, leather, and the reddish earth tones of the adobe styles of Santa Fe.

French country is different again, an **elegant and relaxed** style of printed linens and cottons used for curtains and upholstery. It is a look that manages to incorporate Mediterranean overtones with touches of Louis XIV. This studied, casual look works well in an oak-beamed house in Normandy and a *mas* in Provence, and is popular throughout the world. Scandinavian country is functional and simple, with bleached wood, plain and striped fabrics, and a palette of soft blues and whites.

We look here at designers working out of all these traditions, producing window treatments that are perhaps best described overall as **comfortable**, without being too demanding or mannered.

Country

KIT KEMP

After launching her design career by working with an architect, Kit Kemp met her husband Tim, and together they launched the townhouse hotel group Firmdale Hotels, in London. Kit is responsible for the interiors of all the properties, each of which has been remodeled and designed from scratch. Kit has become known for her unique reinterpretations of the traditional grand, English country house style, both quirky and sophisticated. She has won a number of design awards and her work has been featured in magazines such as *Architectural Digest*, *Vogue,* and *Harpers & Queen.*

RIGHT

A bedroom in a Knightsbridge hotel has a striking lilac-and-purple theme. The bold tulip fabric is used sparingly; and is contrasted with a deep purple lining for the bed canopy and pale lilac linen sheers at the window.

FAR RIGHT

Kit Kemp's bedroom curtains are made from three shades of batik print from the Designers Guild, sewn together in bands—pink, turquoise, and black. The blind uses just the turquoise, which gives the incoming light a wonderful glow.

66 Although I'm known for hotel decoration, I always try to make the rooms look like home. The first thing I do when I walk into a room is to look out the window. I love the feeling of light and freshness and I want a room to surprise you as you enter. Often a surprise can be one of scale, with some element overscaled or underscaled, but I never want people to enter one of my rooms without comment.

For me, curtains are a question of color. Colors now are a lot fresher and brighter, but with a washed-out sort of brightness. There's a new purity of design, with an attention to detail and a wonderful choice of fabrics and materials. You can use trims such as feathers, buttons, leather straps, and metal toggles that a few years ago you wouldn't expect to use on curtains. I see curtains now with less elaboration than in the past, but there's nothing simple about them. Such a style requires a huge amount of thought to look artless.

SIMPLE GLAMOUR
The wonderful design contradiction today is that of simplicity combined with glamour, which can be achieved with fabric. I adore natural linens, cottons, and canvas. Bruno Triplet does a range of double-sided canvas with one plain color on one side and another color on the reverse, or with stripes in different colors on each side, so you don't have to line them.

I like both plains and patterns and I often use plain curtains and bring the pattern into the room elsewhere. I use a lot of borders. I've just had a fabric specially designed, based on the work of the sculptor David Nash, who works in wood that he burns to charcoal. The fabric

THIS PAGE
A wonderful drawing room with luxurious white curtains has one of Kit Kemp's signature valances. It is integrated into the curtain itself, so it gets pulled back with the curtain and does not obscure the lovely arched window.

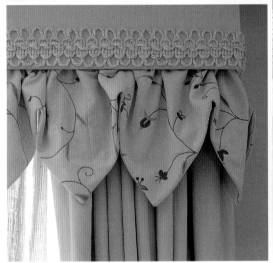

is in these lovely organic colors and I've bordered it in bright lime green and trimmed it with feathers. I use ticking a lot, which I think looks wonderful with pin-striped wallpaper or a black-and-white toile de Jouy. Punched felt has a lot of possibilities, and I've also found a fabric that consists of little squares held together by saddle-stitching. These are fabric options that weren't around ten years ago. I sometimes sew together two pieces of fabric in different colorways and I've made some very successful box-pleated valances out of striped fabrics.

DESIGN CONSIDERATIONS

In a bedroom I'll use blackout blinds that come down at night and disappear during the day. Because I like clear, fresh light I will use sheers in the palest shades of pink or yellow, because in a gray climate they give a room a wonderful luminosity.

Everything is softer and simpler now, even swags. I hardly use tiebacks at all, because I like the long drape, which elongates a room. In most cases, I think you should start your curtains as high up as possible and let them hang to the floor (although not on the floor).

I use valances all the time, but I will often integrate them into the drape itself, so they appear more like a cape over the curtain's shoulders that gets pulled back with it. This is because you get the most light from the top part of a window and you don't want a fixed valance obscuring it. I also now use a lot of industrial fittings to hang curtains with, and I highly recommend a trip to a yacht chandler, where you will find all kinds of cleats, pulleys, steel wires, eyelets, and ropes that look absolutely fabulous. "

You can use trims such as feathers, buttons, leather straps, and metal toggles that a few years ago you wouldn't expect to use on curtains

Kit Kemp.

TOP LEFT
Flat inverted pleating gives this valance stiffness and substance. It is bordered in lime green and brown linen and finished with an amazing feather trim.

ABOVE RIGHT
Cream linen curtains blend with the walls and pale green linen undercurtains bring a little of the outside foliage inside, giving the room a fresh, spring-like feeling.

ABOVE LEFT
A detail shows that the stiffened valance is bordered with a string braid and a trim of handkerchief points made from hand-embroidered crewelwork.

JACQUELYNNE P. LANHAM

Born in Virginia, Jacquelynne P. Lanham was raised in Greece, Japan, and the United States. She studied interior design at the University of Alabama and at Georgia State University, and founded her own design company in 1987. Now recognized as one of the most influential designers in the United States, Jacquelynne has undertaken residential interiors in places as diverse as San Francisco, Chattanooga, Memphis, and Islamorada in the Florida Keys. Her commercial projects have included country and driving clubs. Her interiors frequently feature in national magazines.

❝ I'm a true lover of curtains; I love fabric and I use a lot of it. Atlanta is a very hot place, so you want things to feel cool and fluttery. Here in the South, we like light, but we also want to be cozy and close off the black hole of night. I'm a comfort person—I like to take my shoes off when I walk in the door, and put my feet up on the sofa.

FABRIC COLORS

Decorating is not so much about trophy houses any more, but about being comfortable in a home. It depends on the home, but I love natural fabrics, such as linen and cotton. I also love embroidered textiles, checks and toile de Jouy. Colors are softer now because people's lives are hectic and they don't want their homes to be visually disruptive. I use plains and patterns in equal measure but color is key with me. I take my color cue from the clients. When you're hired by clients, it's like getting a script for a movie, and you take on the character of the

ABOVE LEFT

For the drawing room of this Atlanta residence, Jacquelynne has chosen blue-and-white classic French cotton toile and hung it simply from square-section iron rods.

LEFT

A bedroom in the same home has gathered-heading curtains and a Roman blind made from embroidered linen sheer with satin ribbon trimmings. Together, they look like a gorgeous item of exquisitely expensive lingerie.

THIS PAGE

These bedroom curtains are both innovative and
traditional. There's a calm confidence in the line
of the swagged valances, and the way they are
designed so that the light just catches the
double-scalloped edging is sheer genius.

clients and their preference for color, whether blues and greens or yellows and beiges. My job is to put in place a quality production throughout the home and to make sure that in the last scene there is a happy ending.

DESIGN TWISTS

I love to take a cue from history and I refer back to past styles, take elements of what I've seen and modernize them. I love valances and cornices. On one of my jobs, I took the back rail of a painted American fancy chair as a model and I reproduced it in wood, made a cornice out of it, and hung the curtain from that. In more traditional homes, I will do swags, but again with a bit of a twist. I like to cut them oversized and maybe use a different fabric from that of the drapes.

BELOW

The use of the same fern design on both walls and curtains gives a gentle, all encompassing look to this pretty guest room. The valance is traditional but simple and edged in a darker trim. The full curtains fall over shutter doors.

Curtains use up a lot of yardage, and that becomes expensive. Clients are always amazed at the cost of a pair of curtains—and not just at the price of the fabric. Elaborate treatments require a lot of hand-stitching, which represents hours of labor. And that's one of the reasons why I think simpler curtains are more popular now. 99

BELOW
Both windows and walls are clad in a slightly textured gray chenille, so when night comes the walls blend in with the windows and this elegant dining room is cocooned from the outside word.

Colors are softer now because people's lives are hectic and they don't want their homes to be visually disruptive

Jacquelynne P. Lanham

ABOVE
These fabulous curtains are made from sheer ivory linen, trimmed with a black welt and hung from a square iron pole that runs continuously on three sides of the room, becoming an architectural feature.

LEFT ABOVE
In Jacquelynne's powder room, the gorgeous balloon blind trimmed with a knife-pleat edging on three sides gives the room an instant injection of drama, as well as a feminine touch.

LEFT BELOW
These hand sewn scalloped edgings are lined with a corn-colored fabric. Hand stitching always improves the look of a curtain, and for drapes as complex as these it is a necessity.

" I used to be a fashion designer and marketing consultant in branding, and I wanted to see if I could create my own brand. I thought it should be something to do with the home, because I had been in ready-to-wear for twenty-five years and it was time to move on. So eight years ago, I created Blanc d'Ivoire, a complete design concept for the home, which sells a coordinated range of decorating items.

CURTAINS TO GO

Blanc d'Ivoire is a one-stop decorating store and it's accessible enough for you to be able to change your room simply by picking another item from the range. I took my ideas to India to have them made up there and now we have our own factories and we source all our fabrics there, because they are very high quality and good value, with many possibilities. From the very beginning, we had a small range, but we had everything in stock, so customers could experience instant gratification. Everything was very white, clean, feminine, and easy. I didn't want it to be too sophisticated for people to understand. In the store, I put up displays showing how the

MONIC FISCHER

After a long career associated with the design of clothes, Monic Fischer decided that she wanted to launch her own brand in a more unusual area of the French market—design for the home. She launched a collection of small objects, furniture, and textiles, through her company Blanc d'Ivoire. The textiles she uses are predominantly old Provençal quilts that she restitches in a modern idiom. Curtains are also an important component of Blanc d'Ivoire's range of design for the home, an essential part of the simple, harmonious, and comfortable way of life that is Monic Fischer's design philosophy.

RIGHT
This rustic country bedroom has a lovely fresh feeling. The antique bed takes center stage, and a simple fall of sheer white organdy voile at the windows provides the perfect backdrop.

LEFT
A detail of the curtains shows that the voile is trimmed with a thin dark velvet braid, which defines the outlines of gauzy curtains left to puddle on the floor in a relaxed kind of way.

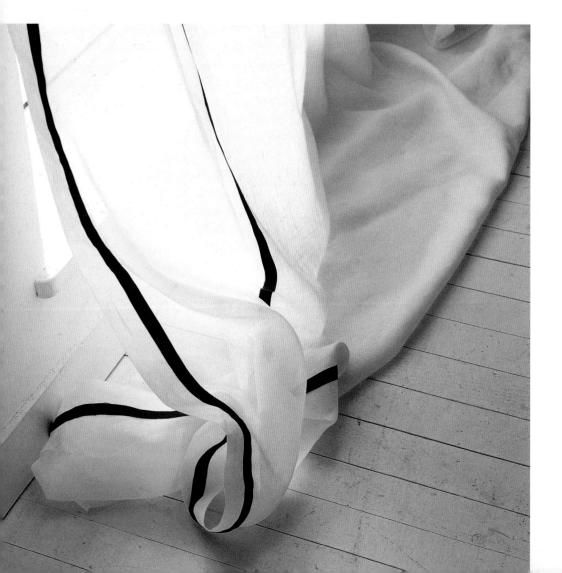

LEFT
Natural linen sheers with tie headings blend with the creamy white walls of this country bedroom. The shawl valance (basically a simple fold over of fabric at the top) adds interest without being in the least bit fussy.

BELOW
These striped sheers in white and beige pick up the colors elsewhere in the room and reinforce the warmth of the wooden floor. They are hung straight, practically as panels, which gives them an architectural, tailored look.

elements could be used in a home, so customers felt confident—they knew when they bought from Blanc d'Ivoire how it would look in their own homes. Good presentation is everything when you are selling off-the-peg.

I saw curtains as disgusting, old-fashioned, heavy, dusty things that had no meaning for me. When we first started, we didn't do drapes at all, and then, gradually, I changed my mind. Now, I'm glad I did, because drapes make up a good part of our sales. I started with plain white organdy voiles, because I recognize that people want to filter light and to have a little privacy, and a voile is a perfect solution. I chose organdy because it washes, it irons, and it is very clean. And then I thought if we were to use several layers of organdy, you might not need "real" curtains at all. I started doing that in my displays, using three or four layers together in different colors. I started to have fun with the mix of fabrics and textures, too, and soon I had curtains and shades that coordinated with the rest of the range.

I progressed from exclusively using white organdy to the introduction of striped cotton, linen, solid colors, and then velvet and silk. Soon, I found that I was mixing the fabrics together for the borders and hems. The effect looked wonderful and it was not complicated to make. My curtains are ready-made with a tie at the top; you just get a rod, tie on a curtain and it's done. If you move, you can take them with you.

LEFT
A detail of the curtains in the bedroom pictured below demonstrates how they are tied tightly onto the white pole and are not intended to be drawn. As they let in plenty of light, this is not a problem.

BELOW
The inset panels and the trimming braid give the sheer curtains in this pretty, French country bedroom a sense of verticality, which balances the strong horizontal lines of the beams of the room.

FASHION STYLE

I don't think people are looking at home furnishing as an investment any more, but are starting to consider it in the same way as clothing. If it doesn't suit them any more, they change it. It's a fashion like any other and should be priced accordingly. Handmade curtains are very expensive, which means you've got to live with them for decades. That's a terrible shame if you find you made a mistake with the fabric or wanted to change your color scheme. I offer an alternative in couture style at an off-the-peg price.

I think the commonest mistake people make is not to be daring enough. People find it hard to imagine putting things together for themselves. In our displays, we do intricate, amusing things with our range and we have a lot of fun dressing the curtains in different ways, mixing and matching and maybe tying up one of the layers to make flounces. You have to put it together right; my concept doesn't sell in stores that don't put on displays. **"**

My curtains are ready-made, with a tie at the top; you just get a rod, tie on a curtain, and it's done

Mischo

STEPHEN FALCKE

Growing up in Johannesburg, South Africa and then studying at the Chelsea School of Art in London gave Stephen Falcke design instincts drawn from more than one culture. He declares himself obsessed with travel, and in his interior designs he loves mixing together elements from different parts of the world. For example, Falcke will mix modern furniture with oriental objects and artifacts from West Africa. He likes to break design rules of scale and theme to produce crisp modern classics that will not date, putting great emphasis on lightness of materials and on the flow of daylight into a room.

" In our South African climate, the window treatment is not the predominant feature of an interior. We have enormous, wide windows, often with wonderful views, so heavy drapes aren't usually appropriate. I use a lot of soft shot or metallic voiles, almost as an extension of the walls. Curtains that tone with the wall allow the eye to carry on across, giving an illusion of space.

BEYOND THE MAINSTREAM

We can put special coatings on windows now, so sunlight no longer rots the upholstery fabrics. The twenty-first century is about homes being functional and as easy-to-run as possible. Silk is the ultimate in luxurious fabrics, whether a taffeta or a shot silk, but there are a lot of wonderful fabrics that you don't have to line and interline, such as linen, voile, or canvas. I look beyond the sample books. I love using denim and trimming it with saddle-stitched leather—it looks quite African. You can take simple, inexpensive cotton and embroider the edge with a wonderful ethnic African pattern. I recently used a burlap with colored wax splashed onto it, that has great weight and texture, and I hung it on simple stainless steel rings.

This is the preparation area of a kitchen in a French provincial-style farmhouse near Johannesburg. The same cotton ticking has been used on the entire width of the wall, giving the house a great sense of unity. In this part of the room, the ticking curtains are used to conceal the area under the sink.

LEFT
In the house's stunning main bedroom, the closet doors are, in fact, curtains with a simple cape valance that match the window curtains, seen in the background. The same plain binding has been used throughout.

There's nothing nicer than layers and layers of curtains: sheers, linens, and leather, for instance, put together. We're doing leather and suede curtains now in wonderful colors, and I've found an amazing fabric in Swaziland made from woven straw. Anyone can go out and buy the most expensive fabric. My turn on is making the most of the least. I did some children's bedrooms for a client and we just took the cheapest calico, made potato-cut prints in bright colors, and hung the curtains on a simple wire. They look stunning.

SHUTTERS, BLINDS, AND SHADES
American shutters seem to have taken over where curtains once ruled the roost, and they're very architectural and simple. People are using screens at French doors, not necessarily louvered screens, but ones covered with raffia that can be opened in little leaves. I love grass blinds, which I always spray to match the color of the walls.

I also love the texture of old bamboo shades bound with string or rope. They go with anything. I recently did a traditional house with lovely silk festoon curtains. I put mock bamboo blinds on the wall above, which made the window look higher and less serious. I always attach blinds just below the cornice to get that vertical feeling. For small windows, like the ones you find in Cape Dutch homes, I'll use internal or external shutters and simple, straight curtains, floor to ceiling, either side.

INNOVATIONS
If you identify a favorite fabric that you really can't afford, I have a little trick. On a simple canvas or cotton curtain I add a strip of expensive fabric about a third of the full width on the reverse side of the curtain. You just see a hint of it when you tie it back or flip the side round. It's like putting a raincoat over a wondrous ball gown—an understatement that I find very exciting in a hot climate.

ABOVE
A beach house in Plettenberg Bay, designed to be black and white throughout, has a cool and calm feel. The simple elegance of the four-poster beds is echoed in the black wooden shutters at the windows. Adjustable louvered shutters are very effective in hot climates, allowing cool breezes to flow through, while providing privacy.

You can use heavy upholstery fabric like velvet, chenille, or tapestry as long as you've got space either side of your window, so it can be drawn back well away from the edges. I did a wonderful nursery in sheer curtains with crystals hanging from the top and the bottom. Impractical, perhaps, but the light play was wonderful. In a Spanish-style house, I hung taffeta curtains from a thin little rod and about halfway down the curtains I added a huge tulle petticoat, so there are massively full curtains billowing out from the tiniest of rods.

Every room should have something amusing in it—that's part of the magic of an interior. I like the excitement of contrasts—something grand with something quite shabby, old with new, rough with smooth. The more into decorating I get, the simpler I want things to be. I'd rather eliminate than add. I'm a traditionalist—but with a twist. **"**

I look beyond the sample books. Anyone can go out and buy the most expensive fabric; my turn on is making the most of the least

Stephen Falcke

BELOW LEFT
Stephen Falcke used a strong, almost Ikat patterned fabric throughout this dining room. The curtain lining material is a delightful, inexpensive check that is designed to be seen.

BELOW RIGHT
A long view of the dining room shows its lovely, informal, contemporary look. Matching shades can be pulled down at night, surrounding the diners with bright patterns that block out the tropical night.

BOTTOM RIGHT
In the sitting room of his own apartment, Falcke has used an unlined Pierre Frey silk red-and-white checkered taffeta and hung it from a wrought iron rod. The white roller-blinds beneath emphasize the twenty-first-century feel of this elegant room.

ABOVE LEFT
Mario Buatta has created a magnificent, traditional American country bedroom here with wonderful glazed chintz curtains and a four-poster bed draped in dreamy voile. The fluid line of the tailed valances is emphasized by contrast fringing.

ABOVE RIGHT
Jed Johnson used pale voile on the small windows of this dark New England bedroom, letting in as much light as possible. Narrow Venetian blinds provide privacy.

COUNTRY PURSUITS

One of the most popular manifestations of country style is the American interpretation and development of historic English country interiors. This has become a grand style, and one of its grand masters is the New York designer Mario Buatta.

Mario Buatta approaches his work from a detailed knowledge of the history of design. "People with a perspective on the history of decoration and design dress their windows wonderfully, with glorious silks, cotton and linens," he told me. "The curtains are made by experts, hand sewn, lined and interlined, and fall to form puddles on the floor, giving a room warmth, elegance, and form. Even a boring room can be totally transformed with a wonderfully crafted set of curtains, which make up for the architecture the room lacks."

Fellow American, Jacquelynne P. Lanham, agrees. She told me that she is "a true lover of curtains. I love fabric and use a lot of it... I love valances and cornices." I think we can conclude that as far as the grand country house look is concerned, the influence of John Fowler still resonates across the years.

Designers working in this style aim, as Mario Buatta readily admits, "to make rich, comforting luxurious rooms with a masterly use of color and pattern-on-pattern, rooms that are great to live in." He is adamant that "there will always be chintzes and silks, plenty of detail and glorious trimmings" in his work.

FABRIC INSPIRATION

Jacquelynne P. Lanham, along with many other designers working in this style, makes extensive use of the embroidered fabrics created by Mona Perlhagen that are influenced by historic crewelwork designs from India. Mona feels that the traditional country look is leaning toward a fresher idiom and has recently produced a range of linen and cotton checks and stripes to complement her intricately sprigged embroidery. Because her fabrics seem to cross the divide between traditional and modern, I asked her how she recommended her curtains be hung. "We use the simplest way to show off our curtain fabrics," she explained, "because it would be silly to torture ornate embroidery that's really meant to hang straight. A rich fabric looks wrong forced into valances, swags, and tails. We use a goblet pleat and hang the curtains from the ceiling on a curved rod, and this makes any window look important. It's a traditional eighteenth-century way of hanging curtains and it works brilliantly with our fabrics."

OPPOSITE

A riot of rusticity from Jed Johnson Associates demonstrates the art of success when designing an over-the-top look. The huge windows are drawn into the scheme by their twiggy crowns on top of pointy valances.

RIGHT

Pattern-on-pattern is a typical country look. In this stylish bedroom, it has been brought up-to-date with checks on the walls and a generous, straight fall of cotton toile at the window.

FAR RIGHT

Sera Hersham Loftus has turned her hand to country here, using a riot of floral fabric and matching wallpaper and a neat scalloped toile valance on an otherwise unadorned window.

BELOW

In a beige morning room, the Van der Voorts, designers working out of Antwerp, have used a Ralph Lauren beige, brown, and cream check to make these comforting curtains. They give them an elegant touch with a smart rope tieback.

SIMPLE COUNTRY

At the other end of the country scale, we see designers moving away from patterned fabrics. "Patterns enclose a room and stop your eye," said Stephen Falcke, "whereas curtains that tone with the wall open things out." For many designers, a modern twist to the style is important. As Kit Kemp put it, contemporary country styles incorporate "a new purity of design… less elaboration… a feeling of simplicity and glamour. I often use plain curtains and bring the pattern into the room elsewhere." There is also a distinct design move toward lightness and freshness in window treatments that incorporate less lining and interlining and more layers.

In Paris, I spoke to Françoise Dorget, who has put together an eclectic collection of furnishings, fabrics, ready-made curtains, and decorative objects in the country style. Françoise explained her philosophy: "My advice is to keep it simple. Curtains that are extremely complicated to make are expensive and, after all, a window is there to receive light, not to hold up a piece of intricate drapery. I mostly use plain fabrics that are translucent, like wool gauze, muslin, and fine cotton, then we add piping or a border round the edge in any color you want."

THE COMFORT FACTOR

Extracting one message from a style that means so many different things to different designers and their clients is not as hard as it seems. The country feeling is one of comfort, however it is interpreted. It's about creating rooms you can live in, whether they are designed to enfold you with pattern, surprise you with dazzling color, or produce a calm fluttering of layers of plain linen. As Jacquelynne P. Lanham puts it, "Decorating is not about trophy homes, it's about being comfortable."

Romantic style is **seductive**, but never vulgar. It's soft without being saccharine, feminine without frills, and swashbuckling without the glint of steel. Here, I have tried to show the work of designers who embrace all facets of the romantic living space, and I have included photographs of my own apartment, because it's a style I love and feel very comfortable with. For me, fabrics and drapes are the very essence of a romantic ambience, yet there are many different ways of achieving the style.

A romantic interior should be **flattering and inviting** at first acquaintance, and then retain the interest through little touches of wit and the unexpected. A sense of mystery and magic is hard to achieve when decorating a room, but many of these designers have been able to do just that, conjuring up a mellow mood with paint, paper, and cloth. But the one thing they all have in common is the ability to know when to stop, before the effects become excessive.

Curtains and wall hangings are an important part of the romantic look. Interiors are swathed in soft, **sensuous fabrics** with perfect little finishing touches. Agnès Comar used a wonderful simile in her interview when she said that for her, curtains are the *maquillage* of a room—and "make-up" sounds so much better in French! Romance is all about putting on the style and making the best of oneself. Romantic also equates with generosity for a style that uses a lot of fabric, layers and, in many cases, a lot of color.

I hope I haven't given the impression that romance is all about looking back to period interiors that take their inspiration from fairy tales, because it is perfectly possible to be modern and eclectic yet still romantic. The layers make the style work for me, as does the abundance; together these characteristics conspire to create **a sense of mystery**.

Romantic

MICHAEL COORENGEL & JEAN-PIERRE CALVAGRAC

Coorengel and Calvagrac met in Paris and founded their design and decoration company in 1996. Their design backgrounds and inspiration could not be more different. Jean-Pierre Calvagrac grew up in France in an eighteenth-century mansion furnished with antiques, while Michael Coorengel was brought up in the functional modern interiors of the Netherlands. After six years of collaboration, they feel comfortable with a style that suits them both and pleases their clients. They describe their work as eclectic and logical, achieving the right balance between materials, shapes, and colors, in whatever style.

" Our motto is: Nothing goes together, but everything has to go together. We come from very different backgrounds. One of us (Jean-Pierre Calvagrac) grew up in big old houses with old French furniture and just dived out into everything modern. The other (Michael Coorengel) was raised surrounded by white modernism and Danish furniture and headed straight for red-and-gold, velvet, and baroque. That is why our style is so eclectic.

PAST AND FUTURE

The windows are one of the most important architectural elements of a room. You don't have to drown them in fabric to emphasize that. Curtains are a very important part of what we do. I would say to people that you should be very careful when choosing the fabric and the way a curtain is designed, because a curtain is the one thing that can make an interior look *passé*.

The trouble today is that everything is influenced by what's in style at that moment—the latest fashion, the latest restaurant, the latest accessories—but it's very hard for good interior design to follow fashion because it is so expensive and should be intended to last.

A soft billow of white silk taffeta at the window filters and softens the sunlight pouring into this Paris apartment. The curtains are edged with a terra-cotta trim to match the walls, which in turn redefines the shape of the window.

A dramatic pair of silk velvet curtains in a shade of deep purple almost blends in with the purple walls. Only the leading edges have been trimmed with a startlingly white grosgrain ribbon to emphasize the shape of the drape.

This room has dark walls, dark taffeta curtains, and dark painted woodwork on the window, but all the jewel-like colors work to give it a richness and warmth. The touch of white in the Greek key-pattern trim is vital to the success of this scheme.

We like to design by thinking in the future and the past, rather than the present moment. Our style is a mixture of nostalgia and forward-thinking. And that often means that the less you do, the more you see. For that reason, we tend not to use fussy drapes or patterned fabric, because the effect is too distracting.

CHARACTERISTIC FABRICS

Our fabrics are often quite sober and simple, but with a luxury feel to them. They have a character that makes them look rich. Our favorites are silk and silk taffeta, which we use unlined to let in the light. There's a lovely transparency to unlined silk that doesn't cut you off from the views outside. In the bedroom of a Paris apartment. We might use heavy, lined silk velvet, however, to protect from noise in the street—and layers of velvet are warm and welcoming

It's very important to have curtains, because they finish a room and give it an elegant touch. We also have to find a harmony between the rooms when the doors are open; because of their visibility. Curtain treatments can do that, not by being identical but by being complementary. One of our recent favorites is a curtain treatment we did in cream silk taffeta with a Greek key-design braid. It's classical, but timeless and those curtains will never age. On the other hand, we will use rustic fabrics for rustic situations. For example, in our country house, we have big black coarse linen curtains, which look wonderful.

We have found a most exquisite copy of an Art Deco fabric made in the 1920s, which is completely embroidered in silk that looks almost like a Japanese kimono. We use that with great care because combining beautifully patterned fabrics with fine decorated antique furniture looks too retro and busy; there's a danger that you will not be able to appreciate anything. It may be nice in a huge country house to have patterned fabrics and antique furniture, but if you use both in a small apartment, it is too much.

ABOVE RIGHT

A view of the salon in a grand Parisian apartment reveals an exquisite play of light. The windows have been left virtually bare, except for the softening drapes of taffeta that make the two windows work as one. Privacy and light control are achieved courtesy of a striped awning on the balcony outside.

ABOVE LEFT

The unlined fabric of the salon curtains is scooped up high into a gilt bronze curtain hook and threaded onto a matching, custom-made pole. The cotton fringing, in a paler gray, defines the lovely drape of fabric.

INVENTION AND INTERPRETATION

The biggest style change occurred between the two World Wars with the advent of modernism. At that time, a lot of decorators started to use very simple fabrics or even no fabrics at all, as a revolt against the overblown decorations of the nineteenth century. After every period of excess, there is a need for purity and change that I think continues today—it's a circle. We find ourselves back with the utilitarian minimalism that existed in the Middle Ages when drapes, which were used as room dividers, were simply mounted on a serviceable rod with metal rings. Historically, there have always been swings between extravagance and simplicity via something in between.

The big changes aside, there have been plenty of smaller fashions. We've gone from Bauhaus modern to the English chintzy look; from the Pucci patterns and cool colors of the 1960s and 1970s to the extravagance of the 1980s and on to minimalism. Now, in the new century, maybe we can take a step back and pick the best of all these things. On an artistic level, there is nothing new. Adolf Loos, the first modern architect of the nineteenth century, said that everything we do is just a reinvention and that we have to reinterpret. It is very difficult to do, but nothing good is done easily. You must pay attention to every detail and you must take advantage of what you have. Do not follow fashion, do not work with busy, patterned fabrics that will date and do not go too far with overwrought designs. Knowing where to stop is a very subtle art. 99

ABOVE

These are custom-made, pull-up blinds of white silk organdy trimmed with white grosgrain ribbon. It's not a traditional approach to curtaining, or a spare modern one, but it's pure Coorengel and Calvagrac style, a timeless mixture of nostalgia and forward thinking.

RIGHT

A door has been removed and replaced with a scoop of the gray silk taffeta that adorns the windows in the room beyond. The rooms are thus linked by complementary curtain treatments.

We like to design by thinking in the future and the past, rather than the present moment. Our style is a mixture of nostalgia and forward thinking. And that often means that the less you do the more you see

ABOVE

A very modern version of a fairy-tale bedroom has been completely encased in muslin, turning the room into a comforting cocoon. Agnès Comar has fixed softly pleated plain curtains around all the walls, swishing them dramatically aside for access to the platform bed.

FAR RIGHT

The window wall of the bedroom has two sets of curtains. The outer set, dotted with fabric flowers, is hung from the ceiling, in the same way as the wall curtains, and is invitingly parted with low tiebacks.

RIGHT

The inner curtains of hand painted muslin are edged with a trim of deep carnation purple. The curtains are tied onto a metal rod with purple ribbons. The room has a fresh and romantic feel to it, without being at all sentimental.

AGNÈS COMAR

Agnès Comar opened her first Parisian shop, where she sold her trademark pillows, in 1971. Now her interior design company attracts an international clientele. With a quick eye for colors and materials, she is able to capture the essence of a wide variety of historic styles, which she recasts for contemporary interiors. She has designed shops, offices, and meeting rooms for Cartier in Paris, London, and Tokyo, as well as numerous private houses and apartments—and even yachts. She believes that interiors should be dynamic rather than static, welcoming yet serene.

66 My style is about *art de vivre*, a uniquely French tradition which I've rethought and reinvented. Its origins are found in the Parisian style, an inspired mixture of materials, colors, and furniture of all periods and types.

THE IMPORTANCE OF TEXTILES

In my opinion, most spaces need textiles, and curtains are a very important element, perhaps the most important. Fabrics at a window are so elegant; they are the finishing touch, like make-up for a woman. They are cosmetics to accentuate the good features and maybe hide a little blemish.

Fifteen years ago, I was the first to use linen in furnishings. I used it on walls and at windows, and that became a strong ingredient of my image. Now I don't use linen as much. I discovered Fortuny pleating, which has a very sensual feel to it. I'm always trying to do something new and different, so when the textiles I use become commonplace,

I move on. At the moment, I'm using a lot of muslin. I like to use muslins of different colors sewn together as one curtain, which gives a very soft and ephemeral look.

The technical advances in fabrics are the greatest innovation in decorating today. What I like is the way synthetics no longer try to ape other fabrics such as silk or linen, but now have their own identity. They are manufactured in a totally different way. And you can use these fabrics in ways you couldn't use natural fibers before. They don't have to be lined and interlined and they won't rot in sunlight. You can have strength with translucency and huge volumes of fabric without weight.

COLOR AND STYLE

I don't use what I would call the neutral palette of whites and beiges. I use colors, not very strong, but soft colors. I take my inspiration from everywhere, and just recently I've been in Naples, a city I adore, and I've developed a passion for the muted, washed-out colors on the façades of Neapolitan buildings.

Curtains are a whole love story with me. The worst sin in decorating is to be boring, and for me boring is being rigidly classic and not using enough fabric. You have to be generous with fabric. Heavy lined and interlined curtains with valances and tiebacks are the opposite of my style, and I think people who want that like to live in the past. My way of working is more feminine, more elegant. I like to live in the future with layers of soft transparent fabric that do not cut out the light, but still give you privacy.

I use whatever fabric I need, adapting to what my clients want. I recently did a bedroom that was completely surrounded in curtains, fabric everywhere, and my client loved it; she said it was like sleeping in a safe and comforting cocoon. Which brings me back to defining my style—I would say it is comfortable, elegant, sensual, and flexible. *"*

I'm always trying to do something new and different, so when the textiles I am using become commonplace, I move on. At the moment, I'm using a lot of muslin

A delicate, ethereal sense of romance is achieved by Designers Guild. Layers of patterned sheers bring sunlight and a scattering of cornflowers right into the room. The theme is repeated on the walls, and the soft colors are picked out by the soft furnishings.

ROMANTIC STORIES

A love of fabric unites the practitioners of the romantic style. "When you look at a space," says Agnès Comar, "you know if it needs textile. In my opinion, most spaces do. At the moment, I like to use muslins of different colors sewn together as one curtain." "Our favorite fabrics are silk and silk taffeta," explain Coorengel and Calvagrac, "which we use unlined to let in the light."

I also spoke to three designers whose passion for fabrics has led them to design their own. Christina Strutt of Cabbages and Roses wanted a fabric that was distinctive and quirky, that looked good in any environment, was easy to live with, and soft. "We started by buying old linen sheets and printing them up by hand with floral designs adapted from various old documents," she explained. "The result is an irregular pattern with faded, muted colors on off-white backgrounds. They are fabrics that can be

LEFT ABOVE
A garden flower theme similar to that of the cornflower room on the far left is found in a strong black-and-white rose scheme by Caroline Quartermain. The window appears to be part of the wall, but the sheer fabric lets through plenty of light.

LEFT BELOW
Unlined lengths of a Caroline Quartermain fabric hang simply from a thin white pole in this bay window, and a smart white roller blind blocks out light and city views. Inside, all is calm and peaceful, with a hint of intrigue.

RIGHT
This is a very modern romantic look from Tricia Guild, thanks to the strong lines of the furniture and the strict pattern on the floor. The gauzy curtains have strong vertical and horizontal orders to link them to the scheme.

what you want them to be, from radically modern to English country house, or to that fashionably shabby chic."

Caroline Quartermain is a London-based stylist who is very positive about the pleasures of fabric. "I'm still swept away by the idea that fabric can be so sexy, sensual, and exotic," she enthuses, "that you can wrap your body, your furniture, and your windows in it. For me, a room without fabric is missing out on these essential pleasures. A fabric is not just a decorative embellishment any more. It is there to shield you, protect, keep you warm, and change the way you feel."

Tricia Guild has been designing textiles for thirty years and is passionate about them still. She says that "when minimalism became fashionable, you couldn't use fabric at windows, you had to use shutters, shades or blinds. Curtains were not considered a contemporary way to use fabric, but I never believed that. I think it's beautiful to use fabric at the window, but not as structured, lined, pinch-pleated curtains. Fabric should be used in a freer way." Caroline Quartermain approaches the choice of a fabric with a completely open mind. "I use whatever works in a room," she says. "If the room calls for curtains made from plain gray silk and old white bed linen, then so be it, that's what it gets. I've used the strangest things; in fact, the most off-the-wall curtain I've ever done was for a Brian Ferry pop video. It was a thirty-three foot drop of the finest rubber, which had a translucency and draping quality unmatched by any other fabric I've ever seen."

COLOR AND TEXTURE

Romantic decorators like color. Agnès Comar is inspired by the "muted, washed-out colors on the façades of Neapolitan buildings" and Caroline Quartermain uses swathes of

A perfectly restrained room for a little princess has swathes of mosquito netting falling from an eccentric crown of twigs and dried flowers. But it is the only fabric in the room, apart from a linen Roman blind at the window.

Cabbages and Roses have created a distinctive, quirky, and individual range of hand printed fabrics, which have a lovely faded feel to them and can be used in all kinds of ways. They look romantic teamed with white, and rather chic with strong, plain colors.

colored fabric "in the way you would hang up dresses or saris or pictures." She likes the idea of being able to change the mood of a room at a moment's notice. "If you want a sunny yellow room, you hang panels of yellow silk over poles; if you feel blue, then you change it." Coorengel and Calvagrac prefer their fabrics to be sober and simple "but with a luxury feel to them—they have a character that makes them look rich."

Tricia Guild admits to having a very acute sense of color. She feels that interior effects are built up by using the interaction between the nuances of different colors. "I think it's difficult for people to know what color they want to live with," she sympathizes, "which is why they often don't use color at all. But color is actually very flexible. You can start off

with a turquoise-and-blue tonal scheme and the following year, when you're feeling a bit braver, you can add a shocking pink. This also means that you don't have to throw things out. I think color has become more acceptable and people are using pattern again in a contemporary way."

BEYOND FASHION

Because romantic style is a mixture of nostalgia and forward thinking, it finds itself well beyond any notion of fashion, occupying a coveted, timeless niche in the interior design world. All the designers I talked to had a very eclectic approach to decorating and the words they used most often were comfortable, elegant, sensual, and flexible. What could be more seductive than that?

ABOVE RIGHT

This new way with sheers is about as far from a twitch of net curtain as you can get. Pull-up blinds swoosh effortlessly into attractive pleats and give the sunlight a color to play with.

BELOW RIGHT

A period room with tall, elegant windows gets the romantic look from the uncluttered lines of its furniture and the generous swathes of carefully draped sheer fabric at the windows.

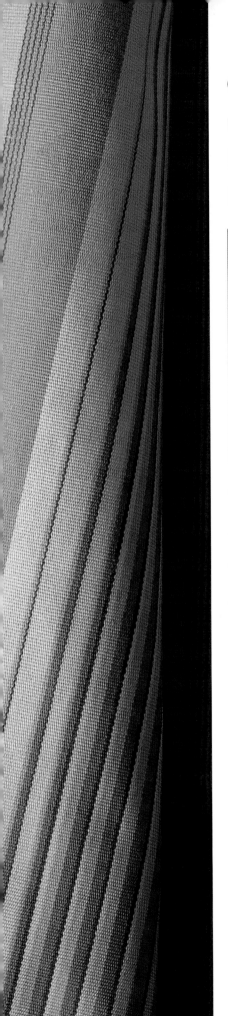

Cutting edge creativity and great skill have never been more alive and well in the interior design business, and it is in the details that they really show. Anyone can hang a length of linen at a window, but it takes a genius to create

a waterfall of crystal droplets to edge it or to make a stunning braid, bound with string rather than silk thread.

In this directory, you will get a tiny glimpse of the many amazing products now available worldwide, but I urge you to look for specialists like the ones featured here, rather than rummage in your local department store. The specialists provide the "wow!" factor in window treatments today. And it's clever details that bring a scheme to life and give lasting pleasure. They can completely alter and revitalize a scheme for the price of a few yards of ribbon.

Curtain directory

4

5

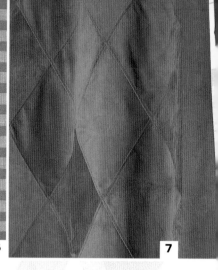

6

7

3

2

1

"I am working on new ways to look at Provençal fabrics, introducing colors such as indigo and deep coral, and I have a range inspired by the embroidery on an eighteenth-century man's vest—very Parisian, very elegant."

PATRICK FREY

Fabrics

I spoke with Patrick Frey of the legendary French fabric house Pierre Frey, who told me that he considers fabric an unfinished product, an ingredient that finds its potential in the way you actually use it. The same design and colorway of fabric can work in a charming country house or in a contemporary apartment. Depending on how you trim it, drape it, glaze it, or quilt it, the result will be dramatically different. Most of the fabric makers I spoke to agree and they enjoy the fact that no two designers will create the same style of curtain from the same fabric—the treatment will always be surprising. There's always the exception that proves the rule, of course, and some fabrics, such as historic archive prints, are so distinctive that it is difficult and inadvisable to go against their own intrinsic style.

1 Detail of a hand embroidered cotton-linen mix fabric from Chelsea Textiles. This is the sort of decorative fabric that could inspire a whole room scheme.
2 An antique fabric sourced by Sera Hersham Loftus for one of her dramatic, romantic rooms. It is a delicate *gaufrage* velvet.
3 A discreet pattern of stars is used to good effect on both curtains and walls in a bedroom by Frédéric Méchiche.
4 Clouds of silk organza, knotted and tied by Agnès Comar. Where doubled over or hemmed, the color is that much more intense.
5 A ready-made chain mail curtain from Habitat in London, the twenty-first-century alternative to the ubiquitous bead curtain.
6 A cotton gingham from Chelsea Textiles, designed to co-ordinate with the company's range of embroidered fabrics. A popular choice for under curtains or linings.
7 A wonderfully soft and supple patchwork suede curtain, a brilliant example of how the choice of curtain fabrics has expanded beyond belief in recent years.
8 A bronze silk by Missoni with multicolored braid inserts.

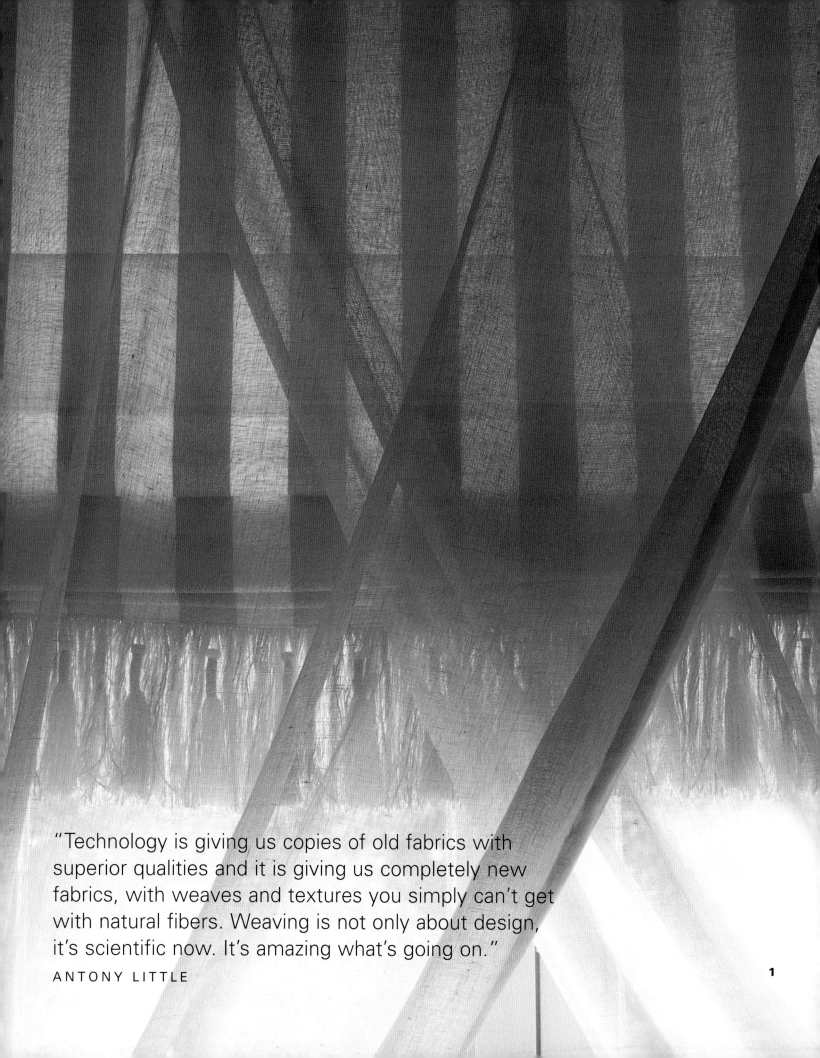

"Technology is giving us copies of old fabrics with superior qualities and it is giving us completely new fabrics, with weaves and textures you simply can't get with natural fibers. Weaving is not only about design, it's scientific now. It's amazing what's going on."

ANTONY LITTLE

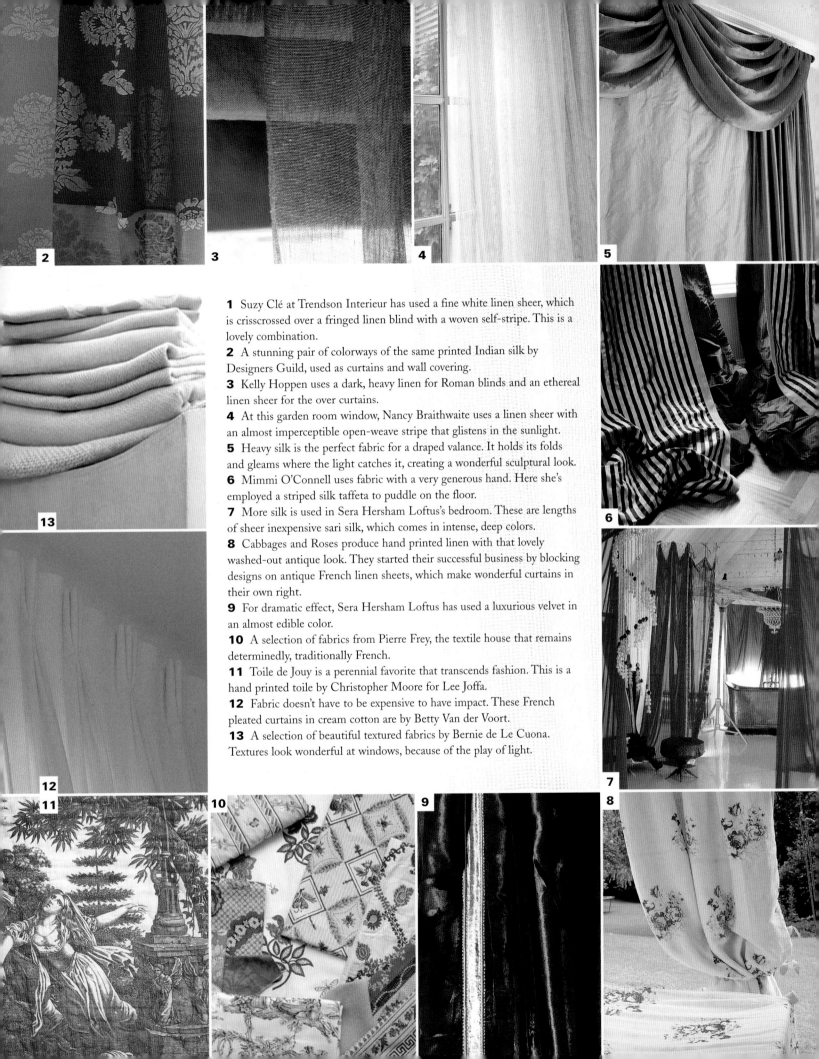

1 Suzy Clé at Trendson Interieur has used a fine white linen sheer, which is crisscrossed over a fringed linen blind with a woven self-stripe. This is a lovely combination.

2 A stunning pair of colorways of the same printed Indian silk by Designers Guild, used as curtains and wall covering.

3 Kelly Hoppen uses a dark, heavy linen for Roman blinds and an ethereal linen sheer for the over curtains.

4 At this garden room window, Nancy Braithwaite uses a linen sheer with an almost imperceptible open-weave stripe that glistens in the sunlight.

5 Heavy silk is the perfect fabric for a draped valance. It holds its folds and gleams where the light catches it, creating a wonderful sculptural look.

6 Mimmi O'Connell uses fabric with a very generous hand. Here she's employed a striped silk taffeta to puddle on the floor.

7 More silk is used in Sera Hersham Loftus's bedroom. These are lengths of sheer inexpensive sari silk, which comes in intense, deep colors.

8 Cabbages and Roses produce hand printed linen with that lovely washed-out antique look. They started their successful business by blocking designs on antique French linen sheets, which make wonderful curtains in their own right.

9 For dramatic effect, Sera Hersham Loftus has used a luxurious velvet in an almost edible color.

10 A selection of fabrics from Pierre Frey, the textile house that remains determinedly, traditionally French.

11 Toile de Jouy is a perennial favorite that transcends fashion. This is a hand printed toile by Christopher Moore for Lee Joffa.

12 Fabric doesn't have to be expensive to have impact. These French pleated curtains in cream cotton are by Betty Van der Voort.

13 A selection of beautiful textured fabrics by Bernie de Le Cuona. Textures look wonderful at windows, because of the play of light.

Poles and finials

With the decline in the popularity of the valance, curtain poles have come into their own, and these days there is a massive choice. Poles that are designed to be admired can be beautifully or wittily decorated and made of just about anything, from perspex with seashells inside to stainless steel. There has been a burst of creativity in the design of finials, too. In South Africa, for instance, I saw wooden finials carved into animal heads; and I've seen others made of hammered metal and cut glass.

Designers don't always look in the catalogs of curtain hardware manufacturers for their inspiration. Many who espouse the simple, minimalist style are using stainless steel wire and fittings from ship's chandlers. Those designers who veer toward a more eclectic, dramatic style are even hanging their curtains on tree branches! All in all, it's an exciting world out there.

1 This studded metal ball finial with a pewter finish by Fabricant gives the rod holding up this bed curtain an unusual accent.
2 A wrought-iron pole with a simple curved end is both elegant and modern. Here it holds a stylish curtain with a tie heading.
3 A stunning crystal finial by Curzon is used to give an unusual lift to a slot-headed curtain in a period room.
4 This formal curtain treatment is finished in a very modern way, with a beautifully simple crystal ball finial that catches the light.
5 A selection of modern finials by Shona McKinney. They are a far cry from the brass balls and lion heads of old.

6 An alternative approach to curtain hanging from Walcot House. These twisted spring clips are pushed onto the fabric panel to form both pleat and hanging system.

7 A selection of pewter-finish finials and ebony-colored rods from Fabricant. The way the metal is worked adds texture and light.

8 Seres of Paris made this elegant pole that has been tipped with metal like a walking stick. The unusual beaten metal finial can also be used on an embrace.

9 Simple wooden poles and ball finials can look very neat and graphic. They blend well with the wall treatment.

10 Classic wooden finials, here with an oak-leaf design, have a timeless quality. They look good with both traditional and modern schemes.

11 A stainless steel disk ring system on a stainless steel, back-to-wall pole. It's a hanging system from Walcot House that is clean, simple, modern, and chic.

"Every room should have something amusing in it—that's part of the magic of an interior. I like contrasts—something grand with something quite shabby, old with new, rough with smooth."

STEPHEN FALCKE

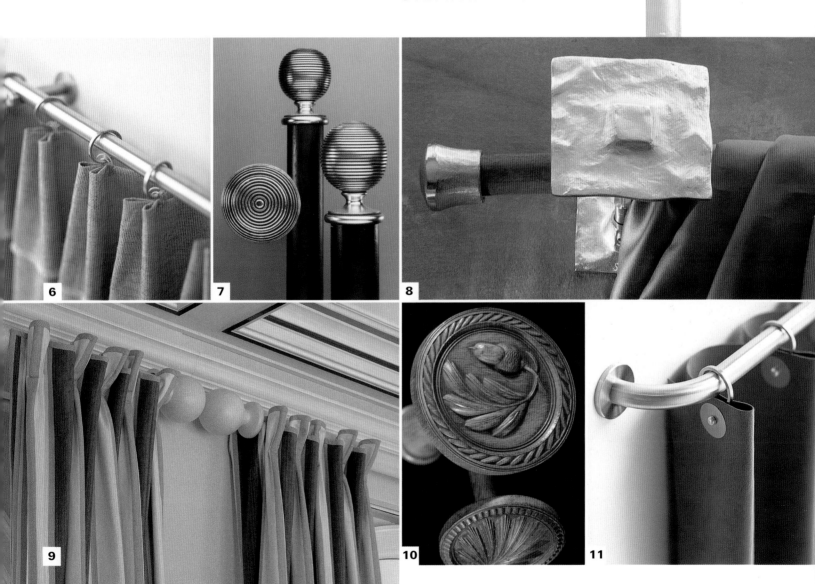

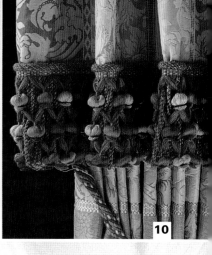

7

8

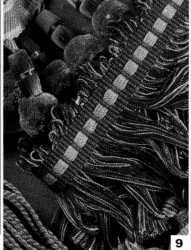

9

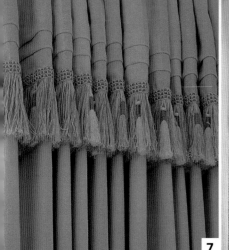

10

6

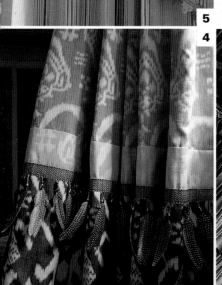

5

Trimmings

I spoke to Annabel Lewis of V V Rouleaux, Wendy Cushing of Wendy Cushing Trimmings and Shona McKinney of McKinney & Co. They all agreed that the worlds of fashion and interior design collide where trimmings are concerned—and they have never been so close. Today, they sell their exquisite ranges of *passementerie* not only to curtain makers, but also to fashion houses, milliners, and shoemakers, and some of the pieces even get used as costume jewelry. If the *passementerie* makers are now at the cutting edge of fashion, it is partly because of the changes we have seen in fabrics used for curtains. On curtains made from leather and chain mail, or from perspex rods, a traditional woolen bobble fringe will look tremendously out of place.

The trimmings that excite me most are made from crystal droplets, that catch the light and sparkle, giving a sunny window a real lift. I also love those made from colored feathers, which are witty, fun, and beautiful.

1 Curtains by Kit Kemp with a beaded trim from Nina Campbell's new range. The beads give the floral fabric a bit of cutting edge.

2 A selection of beaded trims from V V Rouleaux. These would look wonderful trimming a valance or the leading edge of a curtain.

3 This is a beaded droplet trim from Wendy Cushing that is tempting to wear as a necklace. It is jewelry for curtains.

4 Very fashionable at the moment, this feather trim adds an exotic look to these curtains by Kit Kemp.

5 A fan-edge trim on the leading edge and tail of traditional, classic curtains. It adds a delicate texture and a touch of color contrast to the toned fabric.

6 A wonderful example of an up-to-the-minute look: here we have formal gray flannel trimmed with crystal beads from Wendy Cushing.

7 The classic style has not been forgotten. This is a beautiful wool bullion fringe, trimming a traditional pleated valance.

8 Mimmi O'Connell pinned this Mexican mirror to one of her curtain treatments, just like a brooch.

9 A glorious selection of classic handmade braids and fringes from Wendy Cushing. She will color coordinate them with a given fabric.

10 Michael Lewis has used an amazing trimming from Passementerie Nouvelle of Paris on figured brocade curtains.

11 This one-off by V V Rouleaux for Michael Lewis is a sequence of different braids, ribbons, and trims.

4

3

2

1

"You start with the trimmings. The starting-point for many inspired schemes has been something as simple as a bead, a braid, or a ribbon."

ANNABEL LEWIS

of V V Rouleaux

Tiebacks

Many designers are now letting their curtains hang straight to the floor, creating simple columns of fabric either side of the window. Many windows, however, need a bit of swish and a feeling of fullness, and this is where tiebacks come in. Tiebacks can also create a trailing effect at the hem and show off a tantalizing glimpse of a contrasting lining or an undercurtain.

The traditional braided silk rope hitched to a brass hook on the wall has now been joined by a plethora of alternatives crafted in the traditional manner but from unexpected materials. These may include ethnic jewelry, leather, wood, and glass beads—all exquisite works of art in their own right. I have learned a great deal in researching this book, but one of my favorite gems of information is that a metal hook used to hold back a curtain is charmingly known as an "embrace."

1 A traditional silk rope tieback on a lovely, heavy, traditionally lined and interlined floral curtain by Frédéric Méchiche.
2 Double-ball leather tieback with gimp-braided cord from New House Textiles—contemporary materials, traditional shape.
3 Eldo Netto has made a stunning tieback using the gilded and bronzed leaves more often seen on French national memorials. It looks grand but witty.
4 A black leather tieback from New House Textiles. This one looks very modern, with its double cylinder shapes.
5 The epitome of simple country style, a pale rope on a figured, pale, unlined curtain.
6 A simple sling tieback from Betty Van der Voort, made of a contrasting fabric and cut on the cross.
7 Totally traditional: a beautifully made and color-coordinated, silk-tasselled tieback and matching fringe draw attention to the exquisite printed fabric.
8 A jeweled tieback of colored glass beads on a curtain designed by Jenny Amit. The tieback plays with the light that streams through the window.

6   7   8   9

10   11   12   13

9 This heavily lined and interlined embroidered silk curtain from Chelsea Textiles is held in a leaf-design embrace made from *ombré* bronze.
10 A modern leather tieback from Wendy Cushing is ideal for simple linen curtains.
11 A graceful swing-arm embrace holds back this curtain, allowing us a glimpse of the fabulous lining.
12 A decorative metal chain scoops up a swathe of delicate sheer fabric. It looks gorgeous by sunlight and sparkles in artificial light.
13 Two different tiebacks from Betty Van der Voort. She's used a braided string rope for the outer curtain and a simple rosette for the sheer.
14 The tieback as jewelry from VV Rouleaux. In fact, this is made from bone and braid and other elements of ethnic jewelry.
15 A lush and theatrical pair of silk-and-wool fringe and bobble tassels from Wendy Cushing.

"Trimmings used to be associated with traditional interiors, but not any more. For me, they're an expression of my creativity, an art form full of exquisite detail, designed to add instant quality to any scheme."

WENDY CUSHING

14

15

1 Perihan Al-Uzri commissioned these roller blinds from Sabina Fay Braxton of Paris. They are made of the thinnest bamboo, trimmed with silk, and the blind pull is made of real coral. They bring a whole new meaning to the idea of roller blinds.
2 A linen Roman blind by Kelly Hoppen is unadorned except for a wide vertical band in a contrasting color.
3 A delicate blown-glass cylinder pull-toggle on a leather cord, from New House. A jewel to hang at your window.
4 Wooden Venetian blinds look marvellous on expanses of glass. But remember that when pulled up, the stack of wooden slats is often deeper than you think.

Blinds and shades

Blinds and shades are neat, architectural solutions for window treatments—or are they? Today there is so much inventiveness and care going into the making of blinds and shades that you have to rethink their purpose. Yes, they are practical, but they can also be beautifully decorative and subtle. The days of the festoon blind that bunched up at the top of so many windows in the 1970s and 1980s have all but gone.

I've seen the most beautiful antique Japanese roll-up bamboo blinds edged with silk ribbon, and they have looked as wonderful shading tall, elegant windows dressed in the classic manner as they do in homes that are all horizontal and spare. Gone are the frills, luckily. Decorative shades are now more likely to incorporate strips of leather or panels of a contrasting color. Designers are using the new wave of sheer fabrics to make the most delicate wisps of window covering that are practically impervious to the sun's damaging rays.

3

2

1

1 Roman blinds stack into neat pleats when pulled up and look like a tailored panel of fabric when down. A very smart solution.

2 Emily Todhunter designed these lovely sheer blinds with a clever self-adjusting mechanism that requires no yards of cord or toggles.

3 A simple bamboo blind by Jacquelynne P. Lanham gives this sunny bay window a lovely aspect and complements the greenery in the garden beyond.

4 A paper blind with an origami-like complexity of structure has the tactile quality of a sculpture.

5 A string cylinder blind pull from New House and a matching braid give this blind an injection of character.

6 Smart shades from Nancy Braithwaite pull up by means of wide tapes. Double shades add interest and open up the possibility of changing colors at the window on a whim.

7 A delicate blind of stiffened organdy trimmed with strips of leather by Perihan Al-Uzri.

8 A close-up of the blind by Sabina Fay Braxton illustrated on page 180. It's a wonderful idea to mix jewels and silk with a material such as bamboo.

9 A beautiful arched window is often best left alone. This one presented a privacy problem, elegantly solved by Nancy Braithwaite with a sheer blind.

10 Japanese blossom on a Roman blind by Emily Todhunter. A neat solution for a sash window positioned in a tight alcove.

11 A new take on festoon blinds by Jacques Garcia. These sheer stripes soften the windows and keep the sun's glare out of diners' eyes.

12 A huge hand painted roller blind extends across the whole window and has become the focal point in this child's bedroom.

4

"We make a lot of blinds and shutters for modern homes. We'll make the frame to fit the window and then attach panels of bamboo or pinoleum, so the light streams through and makes lovely shadow patterns on the walls."

DOREEN SCOTT

Shutters

Shutters bring a wonderful feeling of calm to a room. They are part of the architecture rather than the decoration and that makes them wonderfully versatile. They can be neatly parked well away from the actual window, leaving an uncluttered aspect, or they can be permanently fixed, letting in light but blocking an unattractive view.

Traditional Georgian shutters that fold into a reveal and disappear completely are a wonderful solution, because they can be used to block out light and provide privacy, leaving you free to indulge your creative whims when it comes to choosing curtains. But most shutters look best on their own. Many of the designers I spoke to favored the American shutter, with its louvered panels that can be adjusted individually for light and privacy. The delight of these, of course, is the wonderful bands of light you get, creating the illusion of more volume beyond.

1
2

"Curtains are not essential everywhere. If I'm doing a light room, I might just use a simple shade or a pair of unlined dress curtains on a pole. I like using American shutters in bathrooms, because you can have a full view outside or complete privacy, just by adjusting the panels."

ALIDAD

1 Fashion designer Bill Blass decorated this dramatic room in the Empire style. To give it a modern twist, he used interior architectural American shutters to control the light.
2 Stephen Falcke has used louvered shutters as a striking component in the dining room of his beach house in South Africa. He has emphasized their sculptural good looks with hand polished black paint.
3 This is a room that patently doesn't need curtains, a huge, barn-like space with light entering from above. John Stefanidis' clever solution here is to dress the windows with fabric-lined hinged shutters that make a bold color statement.
4 Stephen Falcke's garden house is used only on weekends and for parties. He has chosen internal classic shutters not only for their looks, but also for the security they provide.
5 A very simple wooden shutter in a Shaker-style hallway. It looks wonderfully rustic and calm.
6 A corner of a room designed by Nancy Braithwaite. Here she has used shutters with very narrow panels and narrow louvers, and the effect on the windows is slenderizing.

DIRECTORY OF SOURCES

t = telephone number; f = fax number; international and country codes are not given; numbers start with internal area codes.

CURTAIN DESIGNERS

Alidad Ltd., London, UK
t: 020 7384 0121
info@alidad.com

Al-Uzri, Amal and Perihan at AAU Design,
London, UK
t: 020 7583 8000; f: 020 7350 5989

Jenny Armit, Los Angeles, CA, USA
www.jennyarmit.com

Lars Bolander Ltd., Palm Beach, FL, USA
t: 561 832 5108; f: 561 832 9208

Nancy Braithwaite, Atlanta, GA, USA
t: 404 355 1740; f: 404 355 8693
Shirley@NancyBraithwaite.com

Mario Buatta, New York, NY, USA
t: 212 988 6811

Nina Campbell, London, UK
t: 020 7471 4276
www.ninacampbell.com

Suzy Clé, Trendson Interieur,
Mechelen, Belgium
t: 15 205 670; f: 15 210 260

Bernie de Le Cuona, London, UK
www.delecuona.co.uk

David Collins Architecture and Design,
London, UK
t: 020 7349 5902
www.davidcollins.com

Agnès Comar, Paris, France
t:14 952 0167; f:14 952 0167
infodesign@agnescomar.com

Celeste Cooper, at Repertoire, New York,
NY, USA
www.repertoire.com

Coorengel and Calvagrac, Paris, France
t: 33 14 027 14 65; f: 14 027 14 65

Designers Guild, London, UK
t: 020 7243 7300
www.designersguild.com

Keller Donavan, New York, NY, USA
t: 212 760 0537; f: 212 760 0596

Drake Design Associates, New York,
NY, USA
t: 212 754 3099; f: 212 754 4389

Stephen Falcke, Johannesburg, SA
t: 11 327 5368; f: 11 327 6730

Pierre Frey, Paris, France
www.pierrefrey.com

Jacques Garcia, Paris, France
t: 14 297 4873; f: 14 297 4870

Ellen Hanson, New York, NY, USA
t: 212 888 8108; f: 212 888 8133

Nicholas Haslam, London, UK
t: 020 7730 8623; f: 020 7730 6679
www.nicholashaslam.com

Kelly Hoppen, London, UK
www.kellyhoppen.com

Irvine, Fleming, Bell LLC, NY, USA
t: 212 888 6000; f: 212 751 0393

Jed Johnson Associates, New York,
NY, USA
t: 212 489 7840; f: 212 581 0208
www.jedjohnson.com

Kit Kemp, Firmdale Hotels, London, UK
t: 020 7581 4045
www.firmdalehotels.com

Tessa Kennedy Design, London, UK
t: 020 7221 4546
www.tessakennedydesign.com

Jacquelynne P. Lanham Designs Inc.,
Atlanta, GA, USA
t: 404 364 0472; f: 404 261 1792

Michael Lewis, London, UK
t: 020 72624455; mobile: 07958413508
Michaellewis.design@virgin.net

Sera Hershan Loftus, London, UK
t: 020 7286 5948
www.rudelondon.com

Ginny Magher, Atlanta, GA, USA
f: 404 231 1363
gmagherint@aol.com

Frédéric Méchiche, Paris, France
t:14 278 2330; f: 14 278 78 28

Eldo Netto, Travers & Company, New York,
NY, USA
t: 212 888 1900; f: 212 752 3833
www.traversinc.com

Mimmi O'Connell, London, UK
t: 020 7589 4836; f: 020 7823 9828
moconnell@portofcall.com

Gabhan O'Keeffe, London, UK
t: 020 7828 1573; f: 020 7828 1572
gabhan1@aol.com

John Oetgen, Oetgen Design Incorporated,
Atlanta, GA, USA
t: 404 352 1112; f: 404 352 0505

Osborne & Little, London, UK
t: 020 86752255; f: 0208 6738254
www.osborneandlittle.com

Katie Ridder, New York, NY, USA
f: 212 447 6627

John Stefanidis Design, London, UK
t: 020 7381 1311; f:020 7420 5594
www.stefanidis.co.uk

Todhunter Earle Interiors, London, UK
t: 020 7349 9999
www.todhunterearle.com

Van Der Voort, Antwerp, Belgium
f: 14 31 88 71

Vicente Wolf Associates Inc., New York,
NY, USA
t: 212 465 0590

CURTAIN MAKERS

Adams & Co, Wiltshire, UK
t: 01225 865744; f: 01225 866614

Arboretum Bespoke, Hereford, UK
t: 01568 613396; f : 01568 616815

Stanley Baldwin International,
Buckinghamshire, UK
t: 01494 812413; f: 01494 817202

Colleen Bery, Bery Designs
www.berydesigns.com

Len Carter, London, UK
f: 020 7228 6676

Jane Clayton & Co., Bristol, UK
t: 01761 412255; f: 01761 413558

Cover Up Designs, Hampshire, UK
t: 01635 297981; f: 01635 298363
www.coverupdesigns.co.uk

Carl Dellatore, D & F Workroom, New York,
NY, USA
t: 212 352 0160

From the Top, London, UK
t: 020 8671 7629; f: 020 8674 0375

CH Frost, London, UK
t: 020 7737 0451

Stuart Hands, London, UK
f: 020 7373 0068

Heads & Tails, Berkshire, UK
t: 01635 37730; f: 01635 521026

Home-Tex Fashions Inc.
www.hometexfashions.com

Interiors Haberdashery, Stamford, CT, USA
t:203 967 7227; f: 203 348 6320

Ketcher & Moore, London, UK
t: 020 7609 7067; f: 020 7700 3701
Let It Loose, London, UK
t/f: 020 7928 8300
www.thecottontree.co.uk

Ann Lister Historic Furnishings,
N. Yorkshire, UK
t: 01756 760809; f: 01756 760209

The Loose Cover Company,
Buckinghamshire, UK
t: 01494 471226; f: 01494 450939

M'Fay Patterns
www.mfay.com

Parkhill International Ltd.
www.parkhillinternational.com

Pembrice Interiors, London, UK
t/f: 020 8450 6696

D M Philp, Hertfordshire, UK
t: 01923 222363; f: 01923 239925

Ravan Inc.
ravan@mindspring.com

Reliable Fabrics Inc.
www.reliablefabrics.com

John Rhodes, Norfolk, UK
t: 01263 731888; f: 01263 731880

Ruffle & Hook, London, UK
t: 020 7490 4321; f: 020 7490 1646

Sayers & Bays, London, UK
t: 020 7602 6555; f: 020 8201 9986

Doreen Scott, UK
t: 01234 720975

Margaret Sheridan, Norwich, UK
t: 01953 850691; f: 01953 851447
www.margaretsheridan.co.uk

Steven Fabrics, Minneapolis, MN, USA
www.stevenfabrics.com

Angela Swaine, Cape Town, South Africa
f: 21 44 85382

Thompson Schultz, London, UK
t: 020 8993 5196; f: 020 8993 5217

The Workroom, London, UK
t/f: 020 8671 6790

FABRICS

Robert Allen
www.robertallendesign.com

Bennett Silks, UK
t: + 44 161476 8600; f: + 44 161 480 5385
www.bennett-silks.co.uk

Bery Designs, London, UK
t: + 44 20 7924 2197; f: + 4420 7924 1879
www.berydesigns.com

Brunschwig & Fils, London, UK
t: 020 7351 5797; f: 020 7351 2280
www.brunschwig.com

Cabbages & Roses, Bath, UK
t: 01225 859151
www.cabbagesandroses.com

Chase Erwin, Chelsea Harbour Design
Centre, London, UK
t: 020 7352 7271; f: 020 7352 7170
www.chase-erwin.com

Chelsea Harbour Design Centre, London, UK
t: 020 7351 4433; f: 020 7352 7869
www.chdc.co.uk

Chelsea Textiles, London, UK
t: 020 7584 0111; f: 020 7584 7170
www.chelseatextiles.com

Claremont Furnishing Fabrics, London, UK
t: 020 7581 9575; f: 020 7581 9573

Clarence House, London, UK
t: 020 7493 2231; f: 020 7355 4037
www.clarencehousefabrics.com

Bernie de Le Cuona, London, UK
www.delecuona.co.uk

Designers Guild, London, UK
t: 02 7 351 5775; f: 020 7243 7710
www.designersguild.com

Donghia, London, UK
t:020 7823 3456; f: 020 7376 5758
www.donghia.com

Pierre Frey, Paris, France
www.pierrefrey.com

Gainsborough Silk Weaving Company,
Suffolk, UK
t: 01787 372081; f: 01787 881785
www.gainsborough.co.uk

Golding Fabrics
www.goldingfabrics.com

Gracious Home, New York, NY, USA
www.gracioushome.com

Greentex Upholstery Supplies Inc., New
York, NY, USA
www.greentexinc.com

Hodsoll McKenzie, London, UK
t: 020 7730 2877; f: 020 7823 4939
www.hodsollmckenzie.com

Home-Tex Fashions Inc.
www.hometexfashions.com

Christopher Hyland, London, UK
www.christopherhyland.com

Jagtar, London, UK
t: 020 7351 4220; f: 020 7351 4404
www.jagtar-sons.com

Lee Jofa, London, UK
t: 020 7351 7760; f: 020 7351 7752
www.leejofa.com

Kravet, London, UK
t: 020 7795 0110; f: 020 7349 0678
www.kravet.com

Liberty & Co., London, UK
t: 020 7734 1234; f: 020 7573 9876
www.liberty.co.uk

Malabar, London, UK
t: 020 7501 4200; f: 020 7501 4210
www.malabar.co.uk

Ian Mankin, London, UK
t: 020 7722 0997; f: 020 7722 2159

Andrew Martin, London, UK
t: 020 7225 5100; f: 020 7589 4957
info@andrewmartin.co.uk

Metro Mills Inc.
t: 800 631 0244; f: 201 942 4109

Mitchell Fabrics
www.mitchellfabrics.com

The Natural Fabric Company, Berkshire, UK
t: 01488 684002; f: 01488 686455

Nobilis Fontan, London, UK
t: 020 7351 7878; f: 020 7376 3507

Nordic Style, London, UK
t: 020 7351 1755; f: 020 7351 4966
www.nordicstyle.com

Osborne & Little, London, UK
t: 020 7352 1456; f: 020 7351 7813
www.osborneandlittle.com

Paper Moon, London, UK
t: 020 7624 1198; f: 020 7372 5659
www.papermoon.co.uk

Payne
www.paynefabrics.com

Percheron, London, UK
t: 020 7376 5992
www.idv.com/percheron/percheronfabrics.htm

Peter Jones, London, UK
t: 020 7730 3434
www.peterjones.co.uk

Mikhail Pietranek, Royal Deeside,
Scotland, UK
t: 01339 887744; f: 01339 887755
www.scottish-textiles.co.uk

Ramm, Son & Crocker, High Wycombe, UK
t: 01494 603555; f: 01494 464664
www.obelisk-interiors.co.uk

Reliable Fabrics Inc.
www.reliablefabrics.com

Rowley Co.
www.rowleyco.com

Sahco Hesslein, London, UK
t: 02 7352 6168; f: 020 7352 0767
www.sahco-hesslein.ru

Sanderson, Middlesex, UK
t: 01895 238244; f: 01895 231450
www.sanderson.com

Scalamandré
www.scalamandre.com

Steven Fabrics
www.stevefabrics.com

Titley & Marr, Hampshire, UK
t: 01705 599585; f: 01705 598184

Travers & Co., New York, NY, USA
www.traversinc.com

Bruno Triplet, London, UK
t: 020 7795 0395; f: 020 7376 3070

Westgate Fabrics Inc.
www.westgatefabrics.com

Zimmer Rohde, London, UK
t: 020 7351 7115; f: 020 7351 5661
www.zr-group.com

Zoffany, USA
t: 800 395 8760
www.zoffany.com

READY-TO-HANG CURTAINS

Accostage, Paris, France
t: 14 766 7670

Blanc d'Ivoire, Paris, France
blancdivoire@paris-trendy.com

The Curtain Agency, Surrey, UK
t: 01276 671672
www.thecurtainagency.co.uk

The Curtain Shop, Kent, UK
t: 01892 527202; f: 01892 522682

Françoise Dorget, Paris, France
www.caravane.fr

Pottery Barn
www.potterybarn.com

The Silk Trading Company
www.silktrading.com

The Simple Curtain Company, W. Sussex, UK
t: 01403 791818; f: 01403 791293

FINIALS AND POLES

Robert Allen, New York, NY, USA
t: 800 240 8189
www.robertallendesign.com

Artichoke Interiors, London, UK
t: 020 7978 2439; f: 020 7978 2457
www.artichokeinteriors.co.uk

Artisan, London, UK
t: 020 7498 6974; f: 020 7498 2989

Bisca Design, N. Yorkshire, UK
t:01439 771702; f: 01439 771002

The Black Smith Forge, Cape Town, SA
t: 21 44 75 066; f: 21 44 88529
www.blacksmith.co.za

Boulet Freres, Surrey, UK
t: 0208 974 5695

The Bradley Collection, Suffolk UK
t: 01449 722724; f: 01449 722728
www.bradleycollection.co.uk

Peter Brown Designs, Nottinghamshire, UK
t: 0115 9460274; f: 0115 9460228

Byron & Byron, London, UK
t: 020 7700 0404; f: 020 7700 4111

Clayton Munroe, Devon UK
t: 01803 762626; f: 01803 762584
www.claytonmunroe.co.uk

Cope & Timmins, London, UK
t: 020 8803 3333; f: 020 8887 0910

Curzon, South Africa
www.curzon.co.za

Danico Brass, London, UK
t: 020 7483 4477; f: 020 7722 7992

Hallis Hudson, Lancashire, UK
t: 01772 202202; f: 01772 883555

Edward Happley, Suffolk UK
t: 01449 737999; f: 01449 736111

Harrison Drape, Birmingham, UK
t: 0121 7666111; f: 0121 772 0696

Haute Deco, London, UK
t: 020 7736 7171; f: 020 7736 8484
www.doorknobshop.com

The Holbein Collection, London, UK
t: 020 8542 24222; f: 020 8542 5222

Home Depot
(branches throughout the U.S.)
www.homedepot.com

Hunter Hyland, Surrey, UK
t: +44 1372 378511; f: 01372 370038

Fabricant
www.fabricant.co.uk

Finials Unlimited at Christopher Norman,
New York, NY, USA
t: 212 644 4100

The Iron Design Company, N.Yorkshire, UK
t: 01609 778143; f: 01609 778864

Jim Lawerence
www.jim-lawrence.co.uk

McKinney & Co., London, UK
t: 020 7627 5077; f: 020 7627 5088
info@mckinney.co.uk

Gregory Norton, Carleton V, New York,
NY, USA
t: 212 355 4525

Pottery Barn
www.potterybarn.com

Ralph Lauren Home Collection International,
USA
t: 800 578 7656
www.ralphlauren.com

Resina Designs, Bristol, UK
t: 01934 863535; f: 01934 863536

Restoration Hardware
www.restorationhardware.com

Rockingham, Northamptonshire, UK
t: 01536 26000; f: 01536 267699

Smith + Noble
www.smithandnoble.com

Tempus Stet, London, UK
t: 020 7820 8666; f: 020 7820 8777

Walcot House, Oxfordshire, UK
t: 01990 832940
www.walcothouse.com

SHUTTERS

Alpine Shutters & Window Fashions,
Valencia, CA, USA
t: 661 251 1038

American Hardwood
www.americanhardwood.com

American Shutters, London, UK
t: 020 8876 5905; f: 020 8878 9548

Hunter Douglas Window Fashions
www.hunterdouglas.com

Draks Shutters, London, UK
t: 01869 232989; f: 01869 232979

Gulf Coast Window Covering
www.gcwc.com

Lindman, Bristol, UK
t: 0117 961 0900; f: 0117 961 0901

Pinecrest
www.pinecrestinc.com

Seven Day Shutters, Inc., Canada
t: 800 542 2240

The Shutter Shop, Hampshire, UK
t: 01252 844575; f: 01252 844718

Skandia Window Fashions
www.skandiawf.com

Wheeler & Company, London, UK
t: 020 7254 2254; f: 020 7254 2404

BLINDS AND SHADES

A Better Blind
www.abetterblind.com

Accent on Interiors, New York, NY, USA
t: 914 666 8036; f: 914 666 9881
www.accentoninteriors.hdwfg.com

Aero Drapery & Blind Co., Little Canada,
MN, USA
t: 651 255 0007; f: 651 255 0014
www.aerodrapery.hdwfg.com

Auntie Em's Window Covering Center, White
Lake, MI, USA
t: 248 698 0455; f: 248 698 0456
www.auntieems.hdwfg.com

Austin Window Fashions, USA
t: 845 475 0430; f: 847 745 0577
www.austinwindowfashions.com

Blind Alley, Oklahoma City, OK, USA
t: 405 848 0099; f: 405 848 2357
www.blindalley.hdwfg.com

Blind Ambition Window Fashions, Bluffton,
SC, USA
t: 843 815 7750; f: 843 815 7751

Blind Expert, Bonita, FL, USA
t: 941 591 1702; f: 941 513 2055
www.blindexpert-bonita.hdwfg.com

The Blind Man, NM, USA
t:505 342 2000; f: 505 345 7158
www.theblindman.hdwfg.com

Blinds & Designs, CA, USA
t: 415 435 8080; f: 415 435 9209
www.blindsdesigns.com

Blinds Factory, NY, USA
t: 516 409 5959; f: 516 409 9473
www.blindsfactory.hdwfg.com

Blinds 'n Shades Express, Campbell, CA, USA
t: 408 377 0698; f: 408 377 0966
www.blindsnshades.hdwfg.com

Blinds Plus, Springfield, MO, USA
t: 417 881 1821; f: 417 881 1821
www.blindsplus.hdwfg.com

Sabina Fay Braxton, Paris, France
T: 14 657 1162; f: 14 657 0252

Conrad
www.conradshades.com

Desert Window Treatments, CA, USA
t: 760 568 2044; f: 760 568 1986
www.desertwindow.hdwfg.com

Drapes & More Interiors, Santa Rosa,
CA, USA
t: 707 578 0849; f: 707 578 0973
www.drapesandmore.com

Eclectics
Info@eclectics.co.uk

Handy Andy Window Blinds, Tarrytown,
NY, USA
t: 914 946 4329; f: 914 946 4220
www.handyandyblinds.hdfg.com

Hunter Douglas
www.hunterdouglas.com

Levelor, USA
www.levelor.com

Lindsey Blinds Etc., Naples, FL, USA
t: 941 594 5074; f: 941 594 7767
www.lindseyblinds.hdwfg.com

M & M Wallcoverings and Blinds, Sarasota,
FL, USA
t: 941 925 7800; f: 941 925 9709
www.mmwallcoverings.hdwfg.com

Nassaus Window Fashions, NJ, USA
t: 201 261 3500; f: 201 261 0030
www.nassaus.hdwfg.com

Nicky Townsley Designs at New House
Textiles
www.newhousetextiles.co.uk

North County Blind Co., CA, USA
t: 760 944 9056; f: 760 944 6995
www.northcounty.hdwfg.com

Prestige Window Fashions
www.prestigewf.com

Pret A Vivre
www.pretavivre.com

Rainbow Industrial Inc.
www.rainbowblinds.com

Rico's Draperies, CA, USA
t: 916 366 7426; f: 916 366 1645
www.ricos.hdwfg.com

Silent Gliss, Kent, UK
t: 01843 863571; f: 01843 864503

Smith + Noble , USA
t: 800 765 7776
www.smithandnoble.com

Speigel
www.speigel.com

Suncoast Window Treatments, Tampa,
FL, USA
t: 800 683 7862; f: 813 854 1761

Supreme Window, Delray, FL, USA
t: 561 499 1100; f: 561-499-1132
www.supreme.hdwfg.com

Vertilux Collection
www.vertilux.com

Windo Van Go, MD, USA
t: 410 521 1700; f: 410 521 0100
www.windovango.com

Window Coverings To Go, Davie, FL, USA
t: 954 434 4774; f: 954 680 9543
www.wctg.hdwfg.com

Window Creations Fabrics Etc., Cumming,
GA, USA
t: 770 781 8595; f: 770 781 9393
www.windowcreations.com

TRIMMINGS

Abbott & Boyd, Chelsea Harbour Design
Centre, London, UK
t: 020 7351 9985; f: 020 7823 3127

British Trimmings, Stockport, UK
t: 01614 806122; f: 01614 805830
www.britishtrimmings.co.uk

Chelsea Textiles, London, UK
t: 0207 584 0111; f: 0207 584 7170
www.chelseatextiles.com

Wendy Cushing Trimmings, Chelsea Harbour
Design Centre, London, UK
t: 020 7351 5796; f: 020 7351 4246

Pierre Frey, Paris, France
www.pierrefrey.com

The Gallery of Antique Costume & Textiles,
London, UK
t/f: 020 7723 9981
www.gact.co.uk

Remy Lemoine, Paris, France
t: 14 828 2246

The Natural Fabric Company, Berkshire, UK
t: 01488 684002; f: 01488 686455

Henry Newbery & Company, London, UK
t: 020 7636 5970; f: 020 74366406

Passementerie Nouvelle, Paris, France
f: 14 476 9070

Renaissance Studio, UK
t: 01159 732222

V V Rouleaux, London, UK
t: 020 7730 3125; f: 020 7730 3468

Frances Souberyan, London, UK
t/f: 020 7241 1964

Spina, London, UK
t: 020 7624 7974
spinadesign@btinternet.com

Temptation Alley, London, UK
t: 020 8964 2004; f: 020 7727 4432

Turnell and Gigon, Chelsea Harbour Design
Centre, London, UK
t: 020 7351 5142; f: 020 7376 7945

Watts of Westminster, London, UK
t: 020 7376 4486; f: 020 7376 4636
www.wattsofwestminster.com

Wemyss Houles, London, UK
t: 020 7255 3305; f: 020 7580 9420

INDEX

Author's acknowledgments

The designers, curtain makers, trimmings designers, and fabric specialists all over the world who helped me create this book are too numerous to mention. Without exception, they have been informative, inspirational, generous, patient, tolerant, and in many cases truly wonderful. They have never made me feel that I was driving them crazy, although I am sure I often must have seemed like a terrier snapping at their heels. They all showed interest in my work and went far beyond the call of duty to help me produce a truly informative, attractive, and inspiring book. I can only hope that when they finally see *The New Curtain Book* they will feel it has all been worthwhile.

I have to mention Stuart Hands—to whom I have dedicated this book. He has been my curtain maker in residence throughout the book. It was to him we always turned when we required technical information, as well as practical help, and he was always there for us. Bless you, Stuart!

I must also mention Lisa Newsome of *Veranda* magazine in Atlanta, Georgia, who put her office, her back issues, and her Southern expertise and charm at my disposal to guide me through the wonderful talent of the South. Also my thanks to Helen Ballard Weeks and Jennifer Brady for their help, patience, and humor.

Without the kind interest of Wendy Cushing I would never have met Amal and Perihan Al-Uzri and meeting them has been a very special treat for me. Without Annabel Lewis of V V Rouleaux I would not have met Michael Lewis; without Eldo Netto I would not have met Jamie Drake and without the generous intervention of Sabina Fay Braxton I would never have had the delight of meeting Gabhan O'Keeffe. Marie Louise at Nina Campbell's office never gave up on me and nor did Flora at Nicholas Haslam; Tyler of Jacquelynne P. Lanham in Atlanta was a tower of strength, and Mona Perlhagen of Chelsea Textiles was always available for anything we needed. In Paris, Patrick Frey introduced me to many people I did not know and followed this by introducing me to Suzy Clé and the Van der Voorts of Antwerp, who gave us a wonderful and inspiring day. Stephen Falcke of Johannesburg turned his life upside down to help me and Doreen Scott made curtains for me in a flash of her magic wand.

Of all the people who helped and inspired me, I must make special mention of Mary Bright, who was one of the very first people I interviewed. My afternoon with Mary Bright is something I will always treasure. She changed the way I envisaged windows, light, and curtains and I owe her an enormous debt of gratitude. Her early death in November 2002 leaves an emptiness, as she was a unique talent. I am sure, however, that she would want us to celebrate her inspired and talented life rather than mourn her.

Working with Jacqui Small and her talented team has been inspiring. She has, I believe, brought out the best in me and not since Elizabeth David has anyone been able to bully me into doing my best in the way Jacqui does. Her faith in me has made me want to move mountains!

Working with Alex Parsons gets better and better with each book we do together and she makes work a pleasure, as we think in much the same way and we never disagree. Ashley Western has been helpful and patient beyond the call of duty and Judy Spours, our editor, managed to weave all the various strands of the manuscript into form and shape. Karen Howes of the Interior Archive has been available with her great memory for every transparency she has. And last, but not least, the amazing Francesca di Stefano, who only knows how to say yes.

Photographic and designer acknowledgments

All photographs are by Fritz von der Schulenburg, unless otherwise stated.

Front end papers: Mona Perlhagen/Chelsea Textiles **p. 1 main:** Perihan Al-Uzri **p. 1 inserts l to r:** Van Der Voort; Sera Hersham Loftus; Jacques Garcia **p. 2:** Sera Hersham Loftus **p. 3 main:** Stephanie Hoppen/Doreen Scott **p. 3 insert:** Jamie Drake **p. 4:** Mimmi O'Connell **p. 5:** Jacquelynne P. Lanham **p. 6:** David Collins **p. 7:** Nancy Braithwaite **p. 8:** Jacquelynne P. Lanham **p. 9:** Jacques Garcia **p. 10:** Nancy Braithwaite **p. 11 tl:** Stephanie Hoppen/Doreen Scott; **tr:** Sera Hersham Loftus; **bl:** Jacques Garcia; **br:** Sera Hersham Loftus **p. 12 tl:** Frédéric Méchiche; **tr:** Vicente Wolf; **br:** Emily Todhunter **p. 13:** David Collins **p. 14:** Nancy Braithwaite **p. 15 tr:** Nancy Braithwaite; **bl:** Sera Hersham Loftus **p. 16 l:** Jacquelynne P. Lanham; **r:** Bill Blass **p. 17 tl:** Stuart Hands/Colleen Bery; **tr:** Jacquelynne P. Lanham; **bl:** Periham Al-Uzri; **br:** Kit Kemp **p. 18 l:** Frédéric Méchiche; **r:** Stuart Hands/Doreen Scott **p. 19:** Stephanie Hoppen/Doreen Scott **p. 20 t:** Kelly Hoppen; **b:** Coorengel and Calvagrac **p. 21 t:** Nancy Braithwaite; **b:** Eldo Netto **p. 22:** Nancy Braithwaite **p. 23 tl:** Nancy Braithwaite; **tr:** Stephanie Hoppen/Stuart Hands; **bl:** Kit Kemp; **br:** David Collins **p. 24 tl:** Michael Lewis; **bl:** Stephanie Hoppen/Doreen Scott; **r:** Suzy Clé **p. 25:** Mimmi O'Connell **p. 26:** Stuart Hands **p. 27 tl:** Monic Fischer; **tr:** Kit Kemp; **bl:** Perihan Al-Uzri; **br:** Suzy Clé **p. 28 t:** Mimmi O'Connell; **b:** Walcot House, photograph by Ray Main **p. 28/29 center:** Nancy Braithwaite **p. 29:** Colleen Bery, photographs by Andrew Sydenham **p. 30 top row from left:** Mona Perlhagen; Walcot House, photograph by Ray Main; Stuart Hands/Doreen Scott; Michael Lewis. **Bottom row from left:** Stephen Falcke, photograph by Mark Lanning; Emily Todhunter; Serie Rare, photograph by Daniel Podva; Walcot House, photograph by Ray Main. **p. 31 from the top, left to right:** Mimmi O'Connell; Walcot House, photograph by Ray Main; Frédéric Méchiche; Jamie Drake; Stuart Hands; Agnès Comar; David Collins; Mona Perlhagen. **p. 32 tl:** Mario Buatta, photograph by Peter Vitale courtesy of Brunschwig & Fils; **tr:** Jacquelynne P. Lanham; **ml:** Jacquelynne P. Lanham; **bl:** Mona Perlhagen; **br:** Jacquelynne P. Lanham **p. 33 tl:** Kit Kemp; **tc:** Colleen Bery, photograph by Andrew Sydenham; **tr:** Arthur Dunnam/Jed Johnson; **m:** Nina Campbell, photograph by James Mortimer; **b:** Irvine Fleming and Bell **p. 34:** Suzy Clé **p. 35:** Kit Kemp **p. 36 t:** Joanna Wood; **m:** Jacques Garcia; **b:** Jacques Garcia **p. 37:** Arthur Dunnam/Jed Johnson **pp. 38–41:** Eldo Netto **pp. 42–45:** Jacques Garcia **pp. 46/47:** Nina Campbell, photographs by Andrew Twort **p. 48:** Nina Campbell, photographs by James Mortimer **p. 49 t:** Nina Campbell, photographs by James Mortimer **pp. 50/51:** John Stefanidis **pp. 52/53:** Irvine, Fleming and Bell **p.53 r:** photograph by Jamie Bell **pp. 54–56:** Arthur Dunnam/Jed Johnson **p. 57 t:** Colleen Bery, photograph by Andrew Sydenham; **b:** Keller Donavan **p. 58 t:** Mimmi O'Connell; **m:** De Padova; **b:** De Padova **p. 59:** Kelly Hoppen **pp. 60–63:** Kelly Hoppen **pp. 64–67:** Vicente Wolf **pp. 68–71:** David Collins **pp. 72–75:** Emily Todhunter **pp. 76–79:** Mimmi O'Connell **p. 80 l:** Peter Schub **p. 81:** Periham Al-Uzri **p. 82:** Periham Al-Uzri **p. 83 tl:** Nico Rensch; **tr:** De Padova; **bl:** Jean Oh; **br:** Nico Rensch **p. 84 t:** Nicholas Haslam; **m:** Tessa Kennedy; **b:** Anthony Little **p. 85:** Sera Hersham Loftus **pp. 86–87:** Antony Little **pp. 88–91:** Tessa Kennedy **pp. 92–95:** Nicholas Haslam, photographs by Andrew Wood **pp. 96/97:** Gabhan O'Keefe **p. 96 l** photographs by Todd Eberle **p. 97** courtesy of Gabhan O'Keefe **pp. 98–101:** Sera Hersham Loftus **pp. 102–105:** Michael Lewis **pp. 106/107:** Amal Al-Uzri, photographs courtesy of AAU Designs **p. 108:** Alidad **p. 109 tl & tr:** Mimmi O'Connell; **b:** Laureston Castle **p. 110 t:** Cath Kidson; **m:** Joan Schindler; **b:** Stephen Ryan **p. 111:** Frédéric Méchiche **pp. 112–115:** Nancy Braithwaite **pp. 116–119:** Frédéric Méchiche **pp. 120–123:** Lars Bolander **pp. 122/123** photographs courtesy of *House & Garden*/Condé Nast Publications Ltd **pp. 124–127:** Jamie Drake **pp. 128–131:** Suzy Clé **pp. 132 t:** Bill Blass; **b:** Stephen Ryan **p. 133 t:** Celeste Cooper for Repertoire, N.Y., photography by Philip Ennis; **b:** Jackie Villevoye, photograph by Ken Hayden **p. 134 t:** Mona Perlhagen; **m:** Keller Donavan; **b:** Jacquelynne P. Lanham **p. 135:** Jacquelynne P. Lanham **p. 136–139:** Kit Kemp **pp. 140–143:** Jacquelynne P. Lanham **pp. 144–147:** Monic Fischer **pp. 148/149:** Stephen Falcke **p.148** photographs by Mark Lanning **p. 150:** Stephen Falcke **p. 151 tl:** Mario Buatta, photograph by Peter Vitale courtesy of Brunshcwig & Fils; **tr:** Jed Johnson **p. 152:** Jed Johnson **p. 153 tl:** Jed Johnson; **tr:** Sera Hersham Loftus; **b:** Van Der Voort **p. 154 t:** Carolyn Quatermaine; **m:** Agnès Comar **pp. 156–159:** Michael Coorengel and Jean Pierre Calvagrac **pp. 160–163:** Agnès Comar **p. 164 l:** Tricia Guild, photograph by James Merrell; **tr & tl:** Carolyn Quatermaine **p. 165:** Tricia Guild, photograph by James Merrell **p. 166 l:** Karen Roos; **r:** Cabbages & Roses **p. 167 t:** Jamie Drake; **b:** Dina Lamberton **p. 168:** Eldo Netto **p. 169:** Jacquelynne P. Lanham **p. 170 top row from left to right:** Agnès Comar; Michael Lewis; Chelsea Textiles, photograph by Nat Rea; David Collins. **2nd row:** Frédéric Méchiche. **3rd row:** Sera Hersham Loftus. **4th row:** Chelsea Textiles, photograph by Nat Rea **p. 171:** David Collins **p. 172:** Suzy Clé **p. 173 top row from left to right:** Tricia Guild, photograph by James Merrell; Kelly Hoppen; Nancy Braithwaite; Jamie Drake. **2nd row l:** De Le Cuona, photograph by Daron Chate; **r:** Mimmi O'Connell. **3rd row l:** Vicente Wolf; **r:** Sera Hersham Loftus. **4th row:** Christopher Moore, photograph by Henry Wilson; Pierre Frey; Sera Hersham Loftus; Cabbages & Roses **pp. 174/175:** Jim Lawrence, photographs by Christopher Reeve **p. 174 t&l:** Kit Kemp; **mt:** Mimmi O'Connell; **mb:** Stuart Hands; **rt:** Doreen Scott; **rb:** McKinney & Co, photograph by Jonathan Pilkington **p. 175 tl:** Walcott House, photograph by Ray Main; **tm:** Fabricant; **tr:** Serie Rare, photograph by Daniel Podva; **bl:** Irving Fleming & Bell; **bm:** Fabricant; **br:** Walcot House, photograph by Ray Main **p. 176 top row left to right:** Michael Lewis; Mimmi O'Connell; Wendy Cushing, photograph by Stephen Brayne; Michael Lewis. **2nd row:** Stuart Hands. **3rd row:** Keller Donavan. **4th row left to right:** Kit Kemp; Wendy Cushing, photograph by Stephen Brayne; V V Rouleaux; Kit Kemp **p. 177:** Michael Lewis **p. 178 l:** Frédéric Méchiche **p. 178/179 top row left to right:** New House Textiles, photography by David Cook, Blue Shift Studios; Eldo Netto, photograph by Feliciano; Van Der Voort; Wendy Cushing, photography by Stephen Brayne; Jenny Armit; Chelsea Textiles. **2nd row left to right:** New House Textiles, photography by David Cook, Blue Shift Studios; Van Der Voort; Wendy Cushing, photograph by Stephen Brayne; Frédéric Méchiche; Agnès Comar; Trendson. **3rd row:** V V Rouleaux. **4th row:** Wendy Cushing, photograph by Stephen Brayne **p. 180 t:** Sabina Fay Braxton; **b:** Kelly Hoppen; **r:** New House Textiles, photography by David Cook, Blue Shift Studios **p. 181:** Anya and Macio Miszewski **p. 182 t:** Jacquelynne P. Lanham; **m:** Emily Todhunter; **b:** Nancy Braithwaite; **r:** Keller Donavan **p. 183 top row left to right:** New House Textiles, photography by David Cook, Blue Shift Studios; Nancy Braithwaite. **Middle row left to right:** Periham Al-Uzri; Sabina Fay Braxton; Nancy Braithwaite. **Bottom row left to right:** Emily Todhunter; Jacques Garcia; Sera Hersham Loftus **p. 184 t:** Bill Blass; **b:** Stephen Falcke **p. 185 tl:** John Stefanidis; **tr:** Stephen Falcke; **bl:** Nancy Braithwaite; **br** Jacquelynne P. Lanham **Back endpaper:** Agnès Comar.